The PRAYER of JABEZ

DEVOTIONAL

BRUCE WILKINSON

with DAVID KOPP

Multnomah® Publishers *Sisters, Oregon*

THE PRAYER OF JABEZ DEVOTIONAL
published by Multnomah Publishers, Inc.

International Standard Book Number: 1-57673-844-2

Cover design by David Carlson
Cover image by Tatsuhiko Shimada/Photonica

Printed in the United States of America

For information:
MULTNOMAH PUBLISHERS, INC.
POST OFFICE BOX 1720
SISTERS, OREGON 97759

01 02 03 04 05—10 9 8 7 6 5 4 3 2 1

ACKNOWLEDGMENTS

Heartfelt thanks to my editor and writing partner David Kopp, to Rob Suggs for your significant contributions when we needed them most, to designer David Carlson for your outstanding work, and to the whole Multnomah team for your dedication and support, especially to Kim Conolly, Steve Gardner, Jennifer Gott, and Steve Curley for your helpfulness on this project. I appreciate all of you!

CONTENTS

Week Three "O Lord, Put Your Hand upon Me!"

Week Four "O Lord, Keep Me from Evil!"

Epilogue Celebrating the Jabez Miracle

PREPARING *for the* JABEZ MIRACLE

You could call them God's fingerprints. Suddenly you're seeing them all over your life. Unexplainable encounters. Little miracles. Big answers to simple requests that only recently you wouldn't have had the courage to utter. Everywhere you're seeing surprising clues, telltale signs, and unforgettable proofs that a divine hand has touched your life.

It's as if God bent down, heard you pleading for something improbable, and exclaimed, "I've been *waiting* to hear you ask for that!" And things haven't been the same since.

Welcome to "life after Jabez." If you've been praying his simple prayer (perhaps motivated to do so by my book *The Prayer of Jabez*), you know what I'm talking about. You probably have some Jabez stories of your own that you like to share with friends. But now, having embarked on one of the most promising periods in your life, you don't want to miss a minute of it. You want to grow stronger and more effective in your new spiritual adventures. Most of all, you want to experience the miracle in a more personal way every day.

This volume, *The Prayer of Jabez Devotional,* is designed especially with you and *your* miracle in mind. Every page is intended to help you make a lifelong habit of beginning each day with the expectation of seeing and participating in the supernatural with God. You'll find personal mentoring and daily encouragement as you travel farther into your journey of miracles.

Even if you don't have a clue what all this talk of miracles is about, *The Prayer of Jabez Devotional* is for you too. Why? In the pages that follow, I'll introduce you to a man named Jabez and his bold approach to prayer. I'll help you see, perhaps for the first time, the extraordinary dimensions of what God wants for you. You can start today to reach for the blessed life.

If you haven't looked at Jabez's story yet, take a minute to do so. You'll find it in 1 Chronicles 4 buried among some of the most intimidating—and frankly, uninteresting—chapters in the Bible. The first nine chapters of this history book are made up of genealogies. The writer is tracing the official Jewish family tree from Adam through thousands of years to the present, about 500 B.C. That endeavor makes for hundreds of names—most of them unfamiliar and difficult to pronounce.

In mid-litany, the chronicler stops. One name deserves special comment. The briefest of biographies unfolds. In just two verses—9 and 10—we learn everything the Bible has to say about this man, Jabez:

> *Now Jabez was more honorable than his brothers, and his mother called his name Jabez, saying, "Because I bore him*

> *in pain." And Jabez called on the God of Israel saying, "Oh, that You would bless me indeed, and enlarge my territory, that Your hand would be with me, and that You would keep me from evil, that I may not cause pain!" So God granted him what He requested.*

There it is, the story of a man who started with almost nothing but gloomy prospects, cried out a simple prayer, and ended up a man of honor in the eyes of God.

Why is this minibiography so compelling? For one thing, in Jabez's story we find a record of his personal transformation. We see beginning, middle, and end. We even learn why and how his radical turnaround happened.

If Jabez were around today he'd be quick to tell you that his little prayer holds no special powers or magical words. But he would also tell you that if you want to step into God's greater purpose for your life—no matter how unpromising your circumstances might be right now—and you want to seize God's extravagant best for you with all your heart and mind and will, then you're just a prayer away.

Personal change begins for each of us when we cry out to God for *what God wants for us* with open hands and expectant hearts. We make our bold request and wait before our loving Father. Miracles begin here too. And from my own life I can assure you that they will continue as long as you wait before Him with courage and childlike trust.

As you come before the Lord expectantly each day and pray

to Him in both desperation and trust, your own story will change. You'll see new beginnings and new opportunities. You'll think new thoughts. The course of your life will shift.

To help you get the most out of this exciting season in your life, I highly recommend that you make daily use of *The Prayer of Jabez Journal,* the companion volume to this devotional. You'll quickly discover that a written record will help you keep your heart and mind awake to what God is doing in and around you every day. The benefits of this discipline are hard to overstate. Without a written record of your walk with God, the cries of your heart can remain unspoken, the evidences of your transformation undiscovered, the proof of God's amazing answers unnoticed. And that would be a terrible waste!

Remember that you are in full pursuit of blessing from a God who can "do exceedingly abundantly above all that we ask or think, according to the power that works in us" (Ephesians 3:20). To Him be the glory!

May the Lord guide and strengthen you as you walk forward with Him—and bless you *indeed!*

—*Bruce Wilkinson*

And Jabez called

on the God of Israel saying,

"Oh, that You would bless me indeed,

and enlarge my territory,

that Your hand would be with me,

and that You would keep me from evil,

that I may not cause pain."

So God granted him what

he requested.

Week One

"O Lord, Bless Me Indeed!"

The Lord's blessing is our greatest wealth. All our work adds nothing to it!

Proverbs 10:22, TLB

THE FAVOR *of the* FATHER

"Eye has not seen, nor ear heard, nor have entered into the heart of man the things which God has prepared for those who love Him."

1 CORINTHIANS 2:9

I remember the evening my son David asked me for a blessing. Our family was sitting in our living room talking quietly. I had just noticed that David, who was twenty-three at the time, hadn't said much for a while. Then he spoke up. "Dad, I want to ask you a question. Will you bless me?"

His mom and sister stared at him. So did I. His request seemed to drop out of the blue.

"David, you know I do bless you," I said.

"No, Dad. I want you to *really* bless me." Then he stood up, walked to the armchair where I was seated, and knelt in front of me. Then he waited, head bowed, without even looking up.

Do you know what flooded through my heart at that moment? I felt a tremendous desire to bestow on him every possible good thing! Here was my own child waiting at my feet, telling me by word and action that what he wanted most was what only I, his father, could give him.

I put my hands on David's shoulders and started to pray. I prayed for his mind and health and interests and skills, for his friendships and his work, for his ministry, for his dreams for the future, for every part of his life. In Jesus' name, I poured blessing after blessing upon him. And I didn't stop until I was certain that he not only *was* blessed, but that he also *felt* blessed!

I'm sure you know why I'm telling you this Wilkinson family story. Living the Jabez miracle starts in a moment just like the one I've described. You are kneeling before your Father. There's something you need, something you long for with all your heart. You can't make it, buy it, or find it anywhere else. Only your loving Father can bestow it upon you—His divine blessing. And His heart is overflowing right now with an intense desire to give it to you.

Jabez would never have considered coming to God for a blessing without understanding something essential about the God of Israel. This God *wanted* to bless His people.

What about you? Do you feel that He wants to bless you or that He doesn't? You might be thinking, *I'm not convinced that God wants to bless me. I don't think I've earned it. And I'm not really sure He cares about me.*

Today I want you to hear what God says about His nature. Then I invite you to let go of your misconceptions about Him and accept as true what He says about Himself.

When Moses asked God to show him more about Himself, God gave him this revealing self-portrait: "The LORD, the LORD God, merciful and gracious, longsuffering, and abounding in goodness and truth" (Exodus 34:6). Now consider that Moses was one of God's best friends in the Old Testament. He spent days alone in God's presence. So I think we can be sure that God's first sentence summed up what seemed to Him most important to convey.

Ask yourself how your portrait of God measures up to the truth about God. If you see God as stingy, callous, unmerciful, quick to anger, or slow to bless, you are living in a cloud of error that has left you impoverished instead of blessed.

Friend, you don't have to let it be so a minute longer. You can put your crippling misunderstanding down and leave it behind forever.

As you wait before Him today, remember who He is. He is your Father—giving, compassionate, and faithful. And what fills His heart right now is a deep longing to pour out His favor on your life. Will you kneel before Him and ask for His blessing?

MY JABEZ JOURNAL: *What is my portrait of God? Which of God's personality attributes do my actions prove are the most important to me? Which are the least important?*

Faith is a living, daring confidence in God's grace, so sure and certain that the believer would stake his life on it a thousand times. This knowledge of and confidence in God's grace makes men glad and bold and happy in dealing with God and with all creatures.

MARTIN LUTHER

The Royal Life

The Spirit Himself bears witness with our spirit that we are children of God, and if children, then heirs—heirs of God and joint heirs with Christ.

Romans 8:16–17

Have you ever said "Our Father..." on Sunday, then spent the rest of the week living like an orphan? It's a common self-deception. We say we believe something, then prove by our actions that we don't. Even though we're sons and daughters of the King, we can wander through our days like homeless waifs.

I remembering reading about Connor O'Reilly, a penniless Irishman in the last century, whose dream of emigrating to America came true when a wealthy relative bought him passage on an ocean liner. Even though he had a ticket to board, O'Reilly was still worried about not being able to afford meals during the voyage. So he planned ahead. The day he boarded, he used his few shillings to buy loaves of bread, then stuffed them into his tattered suitcase.

For the week the ship was at sea, O'Reilly regularly disappeared into his berth to eat. He ate secretly for fear that other poor passengers would ask him to share—and he barely had enough for one. While well-to-do passengers were enjoying the delicious fare in the ship's dining room, he would stand outside, casting longing stares through the windows.

The evening before the ship was to dock in New York, a man asked O'Reilly to join him for the evening meal.

"Ah, many thanks to you," said Connor. "But I don't have any money."

"What are you talking about?" the other passenger exclaimed. "Your ticket to board was also your ticket to the ship's dining room. You've had three lovely meals a day already paid for since you left home!"

Poor O'Reilly. He spent a week eating stale bread when he could have been feasting in the company of his fellow passengers. The blessings were already there waiting for him.

Yesterday we looked at how much God wants to bless us, His children. Today I want you to realize how much is rightfully yours...if you will claim it. So many Christians I meet are like O'Reilly—they get by on stale bread because they think they're second-class citizens instead of royal heirs. Many Christians simply don't know that something is missing. But a feast is waiting, and it has their names written all over it.

Ask yourself, *How much of the free buffet of God's blessing have I tasted?* You might respond with an overwhelming sense of gratitude for what He is doing in your life. Or your answer might leave you feeling dismayed, even a little cheated. *So much meant to be mine...yet so little tasted!*

Now you know the truth about your ticket. I suppose O'Reilly might have heard the truth about his ticket, but chose not to believe it. Maybe simple disbelief that such a feast could actually be his kept him eating crumbs in his closet.

Are you tired of stale bread? The great news is that you can come inside to the feast. You don't have to be more special, more chosen, or more proven to make it your own. The Bible says, "The Lord's blessing is our greatest wealth. All our work adds nothing to it!" (Proverbs 10:22, TLB).

Our life passage—feast included—has already been paid for by the love of God in the life of His Son Jesus. And He wants you to know and experience His abundant provision as a normal part of your life.

My Jabez Journal: *"God, please help me see what a lavish feast of Your blessings would really look like in my life, and how it would change me for Your glory."*

God never made a promise that was too good to be true.

Dwight L. Moody

HOLY ASKERS

"Ask, and it will be given to you; seek, and you will find; knock, and it will be opened to you. For everyone who asks receives, and he who seeks finds, and to him who knocks it will be opened."

MATTHEW 7:7–8

To bless means to give favor. Give pleasure. Bring happiness. Bring success. So the man who wants, like Jabez, to be "more honorable than his brothers" doesn't say, "Please, God, don't bless them." Instead he prays, "Whatever You do, Lord, please bless me, and bless me a lot!"

We've seen how much our Father longs to bless us, and how completely His rich stores of favor are available to us. But to fully receive these blessings, only one thing remains. Think of it as the key to the storehouse: *We must ask.*

I've posed a simple question to tens of thousands of people: "Did you ask God to bless you today?" Only about one in a hundred say yes. We ask God to bless the food. Why don't we ask Him to bless us?

Many tell me, "I don't understand why I have to ask. I figure that I already received all the spiritual blessings I was going to get when I got saved. What's left to ask for?"

It's true that some blessings come to us automatically. Theologically speaking, when we become a child of God, over thirty things happen in heaven: We are forgiven. We become children of God. We receive the Holy Spirit. We are granted eternal life. And more. God completes these spiritual transactions at the point of salvation—and they're *actual.* Paul was speaking of these blessings when he told the Ephesians that they had been blessed "in the heavenly realms with every spiritual blessing in Christ" (Ephesians 1:3).

But blessings come in halves. What happens on earth for a Christian is the other half, and these are nearly all *potential* blessings.

In other words, God wants me to *want* His greater blessings enough to take the initiative—to *ask* for them—or I'll miss out. It's a golden thread that runs through Scripture, starting in Eden. God puts His best in front of us, then asks us to choose it. "You don't have because you don't ask," James chided. "Ask," Jesus promised, "and it will be given you."

It's a life-changing realization: *The truly blessed life can be mine...but I have to ask.*

I've watched this realization sweep across hundreds of faces. I've seen anticipation, excitement, relief. To these believers, a new level of existence suddenly seems not only possible but also realistic.

But on many faces I've seen sadness and regret. Why? These people are thinking about the wasted years. They feel that they've been cheated or misled. They suddenly grasp the fact that, as a result of their own ingorance or inaction, they've been stuck on the sidelines of God's big plan for them.

How do you feel right now? Have you've missed out on receiving what is rightfully yours? To get a sense of how much you've missed, simply ask yourself, *During the past thirty days, how many times have I asked God specifically to bless me?* Your answer should show you what proportion of divine favor you've either missed or received. Why? Because if you didn't ask, you didn't receive that which comes only in responce to asking.

Change your life today by asking…and asking again. God is scanning the planet today for Holy Askers. He wants to give you your larger destiny. He wants to fill the holes in your aching heart. In fact, He loves you so much that every blessing He gives is personalized to your need to be blessed in a particular place in your life. But your Father won't push Himself on you (do you like people who push themselves on you?). He's full of grace. He wants you to decide what you really want.

In His eyes, the very act of asking moves you from run-of-the-mill to "more honorable." I believe His eyes fall on you today with great delight and anticipation. It was true for Jabez. It's true for you. Asking is the prelude to a lifestyle of miracles.

MY JABEZ JOURNAL: *What are the main reasons I don't ask God for His blessings?*

Asking is the beginning of receiving. Make sure you don't go to the ocean with a teaspoon. At least take a bucket so the kids won't laugh at you.

JIM ROHN

GOD LOVES NOBODIES

For you see your calling, brethren, that not many wise according to the flesh, not many mighty, not many noble, are called. But God has chosen the foolish things of the world to put to shame the wise, and God has chosen the weak things of the world to put to shame the things which are mighty; and the base things of the world and the things which are despised God has chosen, and the things which are not, to bring to nothing the things that are.

1 CORINTHIANS 1:26–28

Have you noticed that Jesus was unusually attracted to people who had emptiness in their lives? And not just sometimes, but often. Losers and loners, the sick and the lame, the weak and the hungry—these were the ones He came for and whose needs He met. These were the ones He chose as His disciples.

When you think about it, you realize that Jabez shouldn't have made it. Into the record books, I mean. He began life as one of Israel's certified nobodies. No fortune. No social standing. No special talents. No promising future.

You'd expect the mention of Jabez, then, to be dust in the back pages of Jewish history, along with Ezer, Koz, and Anub (and his other kin mentioned only in passing in 1 Chronicles). Yet we see that Jabez's life ended up with significance, fulfillment, and honor.

The truth is, God loves nobodies!

Have you ever heard of Agnes Bojaxhiu? She never went to college, married, or owned a car. Instead, she spent her life caring for the starving, the sick, and the dying on the streets of Calcutta, always insisting that her vocation was not social work, but "to belong to Jesus."

You know her as Mother Teresa, Nobel Prize winner and founder of the Missionaries of Charity. Her stooped frame and wrinkled, joyful face became one of the twentieth century's most recognizable symbols of faith in action. Today, the order she founded cares annually for five hundred thousand hungry families and ninety thousand lepers worldwide.

Yet a few years before she died, a journalist asked her, "What will happen, Mother Teresa, when you are no longer with us?" Her answer: "I believe that if God finds a person even more useless than me, He will do even greater things through her."

Perhaps you feel uniquely unworthy of any kind of special blessing. You go through your days feeling vulnerable and weak (although you've probably learned to fake it pretty well). And you go to bed wondering, *Will I ever get it together?*

Let me gently clear up your confusion. The answer to that question is "No." (Same answer for every other human, by the way.) But God has big plans for "useless" servants.

Take a moment to grasp this amazing truth: Jesus is attracted to you! He loves to be needed by people like you and me who are absolutely convinced of our own inadequacies, people who know that without His unmerited generosity toward us, we would be and have nothing.

Have you been letting an exaggerated sense of your own inabilities or status keep you from the blessed life? You *can* change and leave that prideful trap behind. The very fact that you are so keenly aware of your weaknesses and limitations makes you a most promising candidate for God's best.

From the dawn of time, your Father has known you and loved you. He's not waiting today for you to get it together. He's waiting for you to come to Him with open, empty hands.

MY JABEZ JOURNAL: *"Lord, thank You that You have big plans for a nobody like me! Now I beg You to pour Your extraordinary favor on me today. Bring to my mind the "small thing" You want to bless in my life."*

We can do no great things; only small things with great love.

MOTHER TERESA

If you think you are too small to be effective,
you have never been in bed with a mosquito.

BETTY REESE

What's *in a* Name?

You shall be called by a new name, which the mouth of the Lord will name.

Isaiah 62:2

Jabez's mother must have done a lot of things well, but when it came to picking a name for her baby boy, surely she erred.

We read, "His mother had named him Jabez, saying, 'I gave birth to him in pain'" (1 Chronicles 4:9, NIV). In Hebrew, *Jabez* means *pain.* Not only did his name sound gloomy; everyone knew it spelled doom. For Jewish children, a name was taken as a prophesy of the person's temperament and destiny. From childhood on, Jabez would be a prisoner of pain.

Regrettable, wouldn't you agree?

Yet what is most memorable about this man's life is not where he started or what he had to overcome, but where he ended up. Even though he started in pain, he didn't let his experience or his prospects keep him from reaching, with God's favor, for another kind of life. Perhaps God had used that pain, as He so often does, to nudge Jabez into reaching to God for more. Blaise Pascal, a French Christian who experienced much physical and emotional trauma, finally concluded that it had been God's gift to him. He wrote, "Pain was the loving and legitimate violence necessary to produce my liberty."

Take a few moments to ask yourself what name you have put on your life. Have you stamped your heritage or your record thus far with some severely limiting label like "Disappointment," "Not Very Smart," "Unwanted," or "Failure"? If so, Jabez's story has particular meaning for you.

Now ask yourself, *What desirable options have I never seriously considered simply because they didn't match with my negative name?*

God had more in store for Jabez than pain, and He does for you as well. He won't ask you to ignore or deny a difficult past or a limiting circumstance. But He'll never define you by it.

Your Father's name for you isn't Pain or any such word! It is:

- "Chosen" *(John 15:19, NIV)*
- "Mine" *(Psalm 50:10–12)*
- "Beloved" *(Deuteronomy 33:12)*
- "Sought After" *(Isaiah 62:12, NIV)*
- "Friend" *(James 2:23)*

You remember a fisherman named Simon. He left his nets to follow Jesus. If any disciple could be counted on to get it wrong the first time, it was Simon. But one day Jesus looked at him and said, "Blessed are you, Simon son of Jonah.... I tell you that you are *Peter*" (Matthew 16:17–18, NIV, emphasis mine). That new name means *rock*. And along with his new name, Jesus gave Peter a large and important destiny in God's kingdom.

Your Lord wants to say something to you today that will change your life. A word is on the tip of His tongue. It is your new name.

MY JABEZ JOURNAL: *"Lord, what labels or attitudes have I attached to me or my life that might be limiting what You want to give me, who You want to make me, or what You want to do through me? Please show me."*

"See, I am doing a new thing! Now it springs up; do you not perceive it?"

ISAIAH 43:19, NIV

THE SECRET *of* ABUNDANCE

Trust in the LORD, and do good; Dwell in the land, and feed on His faithfulness. Delight Yourself also in the LORD, and He shall give you the desires of your heart.

PSALM 37:3–4

Many Christians have a theology brimming with trust, but a heart full of suspicion.

One morning I was showing a group of men how to use a prayer journal. I had my own journal open on the table in front of me, and I turned the pages to show the men the prayers I had marked off as answered. There were hundreds of them. A big guy across the table leaned over, grabbed the journal, and peered at it in disbelief. "You don't tell me that you're supposed to pray for things you *want!"* he almost yelled.

"That is what I'm telling you," I said. "Why would God want you to pray for what you don't want? Think of something you really want. God will answer. He'll either say yes or He'll say no. If it's wrong and harmful for you, He'll say no. Or if He wants to give you an opportunity to learn something important, He might give it to you anyway. But He'll be delighted that you trusted Him enough to ask."

I encourage you to bring all your requests—spiritual, emotional, and material—to God in prayer. Count on the proven fact that your Father's nature is to be faithful and generous, always seeking your best. He *wants* to give you the desires of your heart. With this kind of Father, you can't be too candid or specific. He won't chide you or turn away.

Great asking always starts here—with genuine trust. After all, you would ask your best friend, not the neighborhood bully, for help. You're convinced of your friend's motives and affection for you. You have established a reason to believe that only good will come of your request.

Once trust takes root in your heart, you are ready to take the next, bold step into the blessed life. I think of it as Jabez's secret of plenty: Plead with Him to grant you what He wants to give you.

You are like a daughter who kneels before her father, hands open, waiting. When her father asks her what she wants, her reply is simple. "I've been thinking," she says, a little hesitantly. "I want lots of things but...but what I want most of all is what you really, *really* want to give me!"

If just the thought of such a bold and open-ended request makes you quake, I understand. Amazing things *will* happen when you pray like that. But if you fear that God will loose on your head just the kind of miserable life you dread, look again at your Friend. Take measure of His character and His love for you. Remember His record of loyalty to you. Let go of all your unfounded suspicions. And tremble instead because the supernatural life of fulfillment and influence you've been looking for is about to unfold!

The secret of true abundance is to want what God wants. I encourage you to repeat that secret to yourself throughout your day. Let its truth rearrange your priorities and change the way you think.

From my own experience and that of so many others, I know what will happen as you move forward in this part of your Jabez adventure. God will prove Himself to you so much that your trust in Him will grow by leaps and bounds. Your desires will be increasingly in line with His will, and you will identify more and more with His values and His wonderful purposes for you and His world.

And one day you will look at your life in happy disbelief. You'll realize that along the way you developed a habit of abundance. Why? Because His power to bless you and to bless others through you was unleashed and unhindered in your life.

My Jabez Journal: *The secret of true abundance in my life is to want what God wants. What are two to three wonderful things God wants for me?*

The purpose of all prayer is to find
God's will and to make that will our prayer.

Catherine Marshall

NO LIMITS

"And try Me now in this," says the LORD of hosts, "If I will not open for you the windows of heaven and pour out for you such blessing that there will not be room enough to receive it."

MALACHI 3:10

The next time you leaf through the Old Testament, look for the God you might have missed. In all those restrictions and rebukes, try to see a caring Father whose generosity is continually thwarted. Try to read the Bible not as a book of laws but as the account of a very frustrated philanthropist.

Everything you want and more, I'll give to you and to your children, God promises the Israelites time and again. "You will be blessed in the city and blessed in the country. You will be blessed when you come in and blessed when you go out" (Deuteronomy 28:3, 6). How much better can things get than that?

For God, limited resources are never the problem. Neither is reluctance or restraint. In fact, like any devoted parent, God must often have to restrain Himself from blessing His kids *too much!* You never read of God saying to Israel, "What do you mean, 'Bless you again'?"

God doesn't keep a ledger in heaven so that He won't overbless you at the expense of someone else. You can't use up your quota of God's goodness. And you can't overestimate His tenderness toward His own.

I love a story that is told about George Mueller, a great man of prayer. It illustrates how I can never be too greedy for God's blessings.

For some reason, Mueller needed to move his family and his ministry to another part of England. All day, workmen carried Mueller's household belongings over the hill and down to the barge that would take them to their new home. As the barge was about to push off from shore, they noticed that everything was safely on board except one thing—George Mueller's favorite chair. But the captain refused to delay his departure.

So Mueller stood on the deck and prayed aloud, "O Lord, please hurry and bring me my chair." The captain, scoffing at this minister who would bother almighty God with such a silly request, ordered his crew to untie the mooring lines.

Just then a man crested the hill, running. He was carrying George Mueller's favorite chair on his head.

This is your Father and mine! Giving—abundantly, lavishly, beyond all your expectation—is what He loves to do. It is His unalterable nature. And He is present with you today, looking for yet another opportunity to bestow His very best.

Is there some concern in your heart, some area where you desire God's favor, that you've always felt was too personal, embarrassing, or silly to ask Him about? Take a minute to imagine how your life would change if God answered that concern. Try to see yourself from your Father's point of view and imagine how much He would love to prove His love to you in this way.

Make this the day you cast away those doubts that limit His goodness. Like any loving father, God cares about your heart, about what matters to you. Nothing you could ask for is too silly for His attention. No nagging need or dream or ambition would put you beyond the quota of good things He is able and willing to pass on to you. Trust Him. Ask Him today for what you want.

And keep your eye on the crest of the hill.

MY JABEZ JOURNAL: *Since I can't possibly use up my quota of God's goodness and favor and desire to bless me today, what should I ask for?*

If there is something to gain and nothing to lose by asking, by all means ask!

W. C. STONE

Week Two

"O Lord, Enlarge My Borders!"

Expect great things from God;
attempt great things for God.

William Carey

Increasing *the* Yield

"Ask what you desire, and it shall be done for you. By this My Father is glorified, that you bear much fruit; so you will be My disciples."

John 15:7–8

Imagine that God's finger is skimming down the phone directory of heaven. Starting at the As, line after line, column after column, He's looking for a name that stands out among all His dearly loved and redeemed people. And where does His finger hesitate, then stop?

Look closely. It has stopped at yours.

Why do I believe that? Because you took stock of your life one day, perhaps not too long ago, and said, "I want more, Lord. I want more *from* You because I want to do more *for* You."

The second part of Jabez's prayer is the cry of the homesteader and pioneer. He looks at his present circumstances and makes a decision: "I was born for more than this." And he prays, "Please, O God, enlarge my territory!" Depending on the translation you're reading, that word *territory* might be translated *coast* or *border*. In life terms, it means the limits of your influence, ownership, or responsibility.

I think we can safely conclude that Jabez wasn't just thinking about growth for growth's sake, or more space at the expense of someone else, or the promise of easy money. Why? Because the Bible calls him "more honorable." To qualify for such praise, the request and motives of Jabez would have to be in harmony with God's purposes.

But Jabez, as a man of the soil, understood that the extent of his land holdings would put a limit on what he could do for God. After all, a given patch of ground could support only a finite number of livestock or size of harvest. To increase his output, he needed more opportunity.

In the same way that pleading for blessing could be called a holy asking in your life, asking for more territory for God can be called holy ambition. And this kind of passion honors your Father.

Can you imagine a warehouse manager being upset if an employee said, "Sir, I want to do more to make this place really hum for the owner"? Can you imagine a mother being irritated with a child who asks, "What can I do to help you, Mommy?" In the same way, when you ask for greater opportunity for God, He responds with delight and favor.

Ask yourself, *Am I asking God for more so that I can do more for Him?*

God is waiting for each of us to grab hold of a greater vision for our lives—a vision that matches His own—and plead with Him for it to come true. To be more fruitful for God, we need more opportunity, and we need to see the opportunities already surrounding us that we have continually overlooked.

No matter how often we ask God for this kind of "more," we can be sure that He hears our requests with approval and with plans for abundant favor.

My Jabez Journal: *Who has set the boundary lines in my life? Circumstances? Others? Me?*

For reasons known only to Him, God has chosen to work through men and women who are willing to make sacrifices for the sake of the "thing" He has placed in their hearts to do.

Andy Stanley

What Is My Territory?

"Lift up your eyes and look at the fields, for they are already white for harvest."

John 4:35

Not long ago I heard from a woman named Shannon in Arkansas who had started praying the Jabez prayer. "I've been given the opportunity to witness to more nonbelievers and to simply help more people in distress than at any time since I first became a Christian," she wrote. Her letter made it clear that she still held the same job, lived in the same family, and pretty much went through the same daily routines. But somehow her life had changed—so much so that she signed off: "I need to start keeping a journal of what is happening. I am sure even I would be surprised."

Shannon is reaching for new territory in her life, and God is answering. You might be wondering what "territory" would mean in your case. Would it mean you have to sign up for more work at church? Start preaching from a street corner? Go to Zanzibar as an evangelist? You may not sense any insight into how to pray or what to expect.

If you are asking this question today, the answer is simple and startling. Your territory is the whole world. Jesus said, "Go into all the world and preach...." You don't have to worry then if you're praying or desiring something God doesn't want. It is His will to touch the whole world. And you need more territory to do it.

The men and women who have touched the world the most for God have begged Him for whole countries. Traveling alone to the Orient, missionary pioneer Hudson Taylor begged, "Give me China or I die!" By the time of his death fifty years later, the missionary group he founded supported 849 workers who had seen more than 125,000 Chinese turn to Christ for salvation.

I encourage you to ask God to show you an entry point for "the whole world" today. It might be your own beautiful children. It might be a needy person in your neighborhood or at work. It might be someone from another culture—across the street or on the other side of the globe. It might be a whole nation.

How you reach your "whole world" is likely to be entirely unique to you. Soon after Glenda, a San Diego children's writer, starting asking God to expand her borders, she got a teaching job with the Institute of Children's Literature. "God has blessed me indeed!" she told me. "For me, writing for children is a way of loving them with words."

Look again at the reports from Shannon and Glenda. I see two key words. For Shannon, it is *opportunity.* She's still faithfully living her life in Arkansas, but she's noticing new opportunities—conversations, contacts, actions that pop up during her day. For Glenda, I see the word *love.* Her writing and teaching gifts are an expression of a central passion in her life—loving kids.

If you're not sure where your larger territory is today, ask yourself two simple questions:

1. What is my overlooked opportunity?
2. What is my enduring passion?

"Open your eyes and look at the fields!" Jesus pleaded. "They are ripe for harvest." Always, God wants to begin with you *now.* He's not waiting for you to become someone else before He can use you. He's not waiting for you to go somewhere else.

Your Father knows you intimately, and He has *already* given you strategic opportunities, passions, interests, and capabilities. These are the starting points for how He will touch the world through you.

My Jabez Journal: *"Open my eyes today, Lord, to see the larger life You're calling me toward."*

We all live under the same sky, but we don't have the same horizon.

Konrad Adenauer

Most people never run far enough on their first wind
to find out they've got a second. Give your dreams all you've got
and you'll be amazed at the energy that comes out of you.

William James

Advance Planning

For we are His workmanship, created in Christ Jesus for good works, which God prepared beforehand that we should walk in them.

Ephesians 2:10

More than anything else, a sense that we already have too much on our plate keeps us from asking for a larger life. *Why should I ask God for more territory?* we wonder. *I can't keep up with my life now!*

I remember the doubt written all over Gerald's face when he was trying to convince me that this part of the Jabez prayer wouldn't work for him. Gerald is a brand manager for one of America's largest corporations. From dawn till dusk, he tracks his time in fifteen-minute segments—and every slot is accounted for. "Bruce, I simply have no more time to give to *anything,*" he said.

"Sounds very promising," I replied, much to his surprise. "Let's see what God can do." Then I challenged him to surrender his day-timer to God's care for the next week. "Ask God to enlarge your borders, and, Gerald, ask Him to let it show up right there on your schedule where you can see it!"

The next week when we met, I asked Gerald if God had given

him a twenty-five-hour day yet. He laughed. "No, but I've had quite a week," he said.

Gerald went on to describe a personal breakthrough. Through a creative application of technology that had never occurred to him before, he had been able to significantly multiply his effectiveness. In addition, during the natural course of his day, he kept stumbling into conversations with coworkers that seemed God ordained. "I'm beginning to feel that a supernatural force must be at work in my life to arrange things according to a bigger agenda," he said. "I don't have *more* time, but God is helping me use my time *differently.*"

Have you ever felt that if you were to really "expand your borders," God would have to accelerate your already busy life?

You are not alone in that assumption. But you should know that God has entirely different ways of enlarging your influence and impact. I can assure you that you'll see God work in at least three surprising ways:

- You'll discover, like Gerald did, that God will arrange circumstances and opportunities that are more strategic for you. It will be as if God has become your Master Scheduler.
- You won't get more hours in your days, but you will discover more effective ways of using the hours you're given. The Spirit will show you ways to double your effectiveness and leverage your opportunities in the most ordinary moments. A walk down the hall at work, a phone call to a friend, a community event—all will

become Jabez opportunities to see God at work.

- You'll notice that as some of your borders extend in certain areas, other borders will shrink. Things that mattered before will drop off your priority list.

Ask the Lord to take the limitations of your time and circumstances today. Ask Him to break them and multiply them like He did for the little boy who gave Jesus the five loaves and two fish.

And get ready for miracles. After all, He's already prepared an extraordinary life *in advance* for you to start on today!

MY JABEZ JOURNAL: *What are the ways that I've been letting the ticking of the clock drown out the roar of eternity?*

Never tell a young person that anything cannot be done.
God may have been waiting centuries for someone
ignorant enough of the impossible to do that very thing.

JOHN ANDREW HOLMES

THE FACE *of* FEAR

"Have I not commanded you? Be strong and of good courage; do not be afraid, nor be dismayed, for the LORD your God is with you wherever you go."

JOSHUA 1:9

Have you noticed how often the subject of fear comes up when God is preparing His people to take more ground for Him?

You'll find it in God's conversations with Abraham, Jacob, Moses, Gideon, and David. You'll find it, too, in Jesus' conversations with the disciples. "Don't be afraid," He told them often after the resurrection. Then when he was sending them off to turn the world upside down, He said, "I am with you always, even to the end of the age" (Matthew 28:20).

Feelings of fear and stepping across a new frontier go together, don't they? God spoke the words in today's verse to Joshua at a key moment in his life. The next day he would be leading the Israelite army across the Jordan. Just across that river lay the Promised Land, and every inch of it would be contested by a superior foe. But God knew that Joshua's fears, and the faulty beliefs they were based on, were the first enemy he would face in the campaign, and perhaps the most dangerous.

I've noticed that the fears that hinder us from doing more for God are nearly always based on an untruth—a misleading assumption about ourselves or our circumstances or God—that is keeping us from God's best.

For example, a fear that many slip into is based on a string of lies: *My performance depends on me. My security depends on me. My success depends on me.* Even though our emotions are triggered by these lies, do we *really* believe them? No. In fact, we have a lot of reason to believe otherwise. God's personal promises, His trustworthiness through the ages, and our life experiences all add up to a string of undeniable truths: *Where God leads me, He provides. What God requires, He empowers me to do.* And, *It's a lot smarter to depend on God than to depend on me.*

Here's a common lie about fear that keeps many from moving forward for God: *I wouldn't feel afraid if I were doing what God wanted me to do. So since I feel fear, God must not be in this.*

Could this kind of fear be cutting you off from the blessings and influence you so deeply desire? Look again, and you'll see the root deceptions at work:

- You're basing your conclusions on how you feel.
- You're equating unwanted feelings of fear with a bad idea.
- You're concluding that the presence of fear equals the absence of courage or faith to proceed.

And those are all lies!

God cares today about your concerns and anxieties and faltering heart, but He doesn't want those feelings to determine what you believe, or what you do, or who you become. Jesus told His followers, "Do not be afraid, little flock, for your Father has been pleased to give you the Kingdom" (Luke 12:32).

Joshua would tell you that no matter what you're feeling, the truth is what matters: You're not alone. God will fight for you. And you can go ahead in spite of any fears you might have to take the new ground God is giving you.

My Jabez Journal: *What fear is stopping me today? And what lie is giving that fear so much power over me? The next time I face this fear, what should I do?*

Don't be afraid to take a big step.
You can't cross a chasm in two small jumps.

David Lloyd George

For God has not given us a spirit of fear,
but of power and of love and of a sound mind.

2 Timothy 1:7

COMFORT ZONES

"Now therefore, give me this mountain of which the LORD spoke in that day; for you heard in that day how the Anakim were there, and that the cities were great and fortified. It may be that the LORD will be with me, and I shall be able to drive them out as the LORD said." And Joshua blessed him, and gave Hebron to Caleb the son of Jephunneh as an inheritance.

JOSHUA 14:12–13

When I ask Christians in North America what might be holding them back from asking God for more ministry, I hear a recurring, continent-sized reason. "If I tell God I'll do anything for Him, go anywhere," they say, "I know He'll send me to Africa! I just don't think I could handle the discomforts and the dangers there."

That one word—*Africa*—seems to stand for the most terrifying fate they could imagine, and the very fate their "loving" God will likely bestow on them *if* they give Him the least opportunity. (Interestingly, when I ask the same question to audiences in Africa, they have their own big reason for holding out on God—New York! "Why, it's so dangerous there!" they exclaim.)

Does this line of thinking sound familiar? If so, you're normal. We're all wary of getting out of our comfort zones. Inside our hearts lives a fearful child who always wants to keep things safe.

That's why I love the story of Caleb. In today's verse, he's addressing his old friend and comrade-in-arms, Joshua. They've faced a lot of hardships together since leaving Egypt. Forty-five years earlier they were among the group of commandos Moses sent to spy out the land—and the only two who trusted that God would help Israel win the Promised Land against enormous odds. Now, both men are in their eighties, most of Canaan has been conquered, and General Joshua is busy parceling out real estate to the clans of Israel.

But Caleb still wants the land promised him by Moses for his bravery as a spy and because "he wholly followed the Lord" (Joshua 14:9). In fact, he intends to get it for himself and his family even if he has to fight for it. Which is exactly what happens. After receiving Joshua's blessing, Caleb leads successful assaults on the mountain stronghold of Hebron and another city as well. At eighty-five! No wonder this man rates as one of the greatest warriors in Israel's history.

Caleb reminds me of an important truth about comfort zones: *If you want to claim God's best for you, don't plan on spending too much time in your present comfort zone.*

Have you noticed that comfort zones are always fluid? By that I mean you move from a smaller comfort zone to a larger one. Your next comfort zone is larger still. In each new zone, you feel the same amount of safety or threat, but your zone has grown.

In the process of taking more territory in your life, you will always move through predictable cycles of comfort, discomfort, and comfort again:

- Comfort—You have feelings of rest and security as you occupy your territory. With God's help, you see a mountain to take.
- Discomfort—You have feelings of fear, being overwhelmed, and wanting to retreat from the new challenge. Yet with God's help, you "take courage"—and take the mountain.
- Comfort—You have feelings of exhilaration, greater faith, and thankfulness…and a return to rest.

You've seen this cycle played out as you've grown through different levels of athletic, social, or professional accomplishment. Perhaps you've also seen it in your ministry growth—for example, you started working in the church nursery, then you helped in junior church, and now you lead a rambunctious class of twelve-year-olds and love every minute of it. At each stage, you moved through discomfort to comfort—and became a prime candidate for discomfort again in a place of greater service.

Where do you think you might be in the comfort/discomfort cycle? What does that tell you about where God might be leading you next?

Countless Christians allow fear to stop them in their tracks *because they assume that the feeling of fear is a red light from God* (and a feeling of courage is a green light). Yet when we feel fear in following God, we are told to "take courage." In fact, those who achieve greatness for God run toward the discomfort zone because that's the primary place where borders expand.

When you follow the Lord in ministry, God always comes knocking with a bigger idea. You see, He wants all His sons and daughters to be Calebs and Jabezes! And one day God's idea for you will be so big that going to Africa or to New York will seem like just another amazing opportunity for you to watch Him keep His promises.

My Jabez Journal: *"Lord, what mountain do You want me to ask for in Your name today?"*

A ship in harbor is safe, but that is not what ships are built for.

William Shedd

They that wait upon the Lord shall renew their strength;
they shall mount up with wings as eagles; they shall run,
and not be weary; and they shall walk, and not faint.

Isaiah 40:31, KJV

Jabez Appointments

Always be ready to give a defense to everyone who asks you a reason for the hope that is in you, with meekness and fear.

1 Peter 3:15

It was just another day on a Missouri highway until Jeff started to pray. What he prayed for on this particular day was larger borders. What he had in mind was to become God's man in the coming year on his production team at the assembly plant. What God had in mind was a hitchhiker beside the road.

"I can't say I usually pick up hitchhikers, Bruce," he told me later. "But I had just asked God to expand my territory. There I was driving my truck, and suddenly out of the corner of my eye, I noticed a guy who needed a ride."

Just in case the man beside the road was his Jabez appointment, Jeff pulled over, and the hitchhiker jumped in. As Jeff pulled back onto the highway, his passenger said something Jeff will always remember.

"I'm not a prayin' man," the hitchhiker began, "but I figured that only a Christian would stop for me, so I asked God for help."

Lord, You're amazing! Jeff nearly shouted to himself. Now he was certain that he hadn't missed his appointment with a miracle. And he was right. Before the next gas station, Jeff had led his new acquaintance into a personal, saving encounter with Christ.

"Now when I ask God for new territory," says Jeff, "I ask for better eyes to see it coming—and better peripheral vision too!"

One of the most exciting aspects of pursuing God's blessings is learning to see what He is doing around you at all times. Jesus said, "My Father is always at his work" (John 5:17, NIV). Always. Are you prepared for that today? Watching for it? Do you even know what to look for?

You can begin today to see God "at His work." Here are five key breakthrough realizations that have helped me see and keep my appointments for God:

1. *Everyone has a need.* Jesus was moved by compassion as He looked at crowds. Why? Because He could see into the hearts of every person, and He knew that He had what they most needed. By the power of the Holy Spirit, I am Christ's representative in my needy corner of the world. Every person I meet today is an encounter waiting to happen.
2. *God wants to use me now.* The problem is never God's ability to meet a need through me; it's my willingness to be used by Him. Isaiah heard God's voice asking, "Whom shall I send, and who will go for Us?" (Isaiah 6:8). Even though Isaiah was keenly aware of his shortcomings, he responded immediately: "Here am I! Send me" (v. 8).

God is always looking for people who are wide awake for a divine appointment. If I could glance at God's schedule planner for how He intends to use me, I would see that my appointment is nearly always *right now!*

3. *God's schedule for me is full of surprises.* I have what I call "left field days" on a regular basis—those are the days when God's plan for me comes flying out of left field and takes me by surprise. As Jeff realized, it takes peripheral vision as much as looking straight ahead. "Never make the blunder of trying to forecast the way God is going to answer your prayers," advised Oswald Chambers.

In the first half of Acts, when the ways of the Holy Spirit seem so surprising to Jesus' disciples, they had to learn over and over to be ready for anything. Heal a lame man? Preach to thousands? Jump in a chariot with an Ethiopian? Eat pork with a Gentile seeker? Yes! It's all in a day's work in this awesome adventure of being part of God's movement on earth.

4. *The problem isn't the needs of others or* the desire or ability of God to meet those needs, but my readiness. That's why I routinely pray, "Lord, let me see what You want to do in me and through me today! Don't let me miss it!" And I've learned that "my Father is always at His work" right where I am—in an airport, in a coffee shop, in a hallway at work, in my front yard, in an elevator….

5. *Therefore, it's always right to ask,* "How can I help you?" I call this my Jabez question. So often, the words seem

> small, plain, and weak. Yet God uses this simple question over and over to initiate an encounter. Try it. When you ask a person, "How can I help you?" your Jabez appointment will look at you, perhaps with some surprise or puzzlement, then proceed to reveal exactly why God has brought you together.

Today, Your Father is at work. And if you open your eyes and your mouth for Him today, you'll meet a miracle with your name written all over it.

My Jabez Journal: *On what occasion in my past have I felt most sure that I was keeping an appointment with someone for God? What did God do through me? What can I learn from it?*

"I have come into this world, that those who do not see may see."

John 9:39

THE SIMPLE TRUTH

For I know the thoughts that I think toward you, says the LORD, thoughts of peace and not of evil, to give you a future and a hope.

JEREMIAH 29:11

Life change takes place when you change how you think. Truth is wasted in our lives if we don't put it to work to accomplish what God wants. Jesus promised, "You shall know the truth, and the truth shall make you free" (John 8:32). Yet most of us are only beginners at experiencing God's blessings because we haven't let the truth set us free by changing what we think and do.

I hope you are looking at the boundary lines of your life and thinking in new ways.

Here's one simple truth that can change you today: *God wants you to urgently desire a larger life with more opportunities to serve Him.*

Here's another simple truth: *No matter how much God wants to expand your territory, He still waits for you to sincerely want it and plead for it.*

So urgently ask! Ask Him for a Jabez family—more honorable, more blessed, more influential—to the utter shock of everyone around you! Ask Him for more business contacts, more accounts, higher profits, greater respect and influence in your professional arena, and more opportunities for you to ask, "How may I help you?"

You see, God wants to flood your life with miracles. The

miracles will be entirely by His power, but to make this life happen, you have to do something.

Consider what God said to His people about what they would have to do to claim the Promised Land:

- To Abraham, He said, *"It's already yours,* but you have to start a journey away from the comfortable and known, and toward the new and unknown."
- To Moses, He said, *"It's already yours,* but you have to step up to leadership, service, and ministry."
- To Joshua, He said, *"It's already yours,* but you have to fight for it."
- To the people upon entering the Promised Land, He said, *"It's already yours,* but you have to follow Me in patient trust and wholehearted obedience."
- To the people after they took possession: *"It's already yours,* but you must believe and act upon the truth to keep it."

Is God saying any of these things to you today? God has a huge sphere of influence ready for you, but you must act upon truths you already know to take it, or it will never be yours.

An acquaintance of mine took his teenage son, Aaron, on a father-son vacation to Victoria Falls in Zimbabwe, Africa. Peter thought that he and Aaron could make a memory of a lifetime together hiking around the world's mightiest waterfall. But once they had seen the falls, what caught the teenager's attention was the opportunity to jump off the high, single-span Victoria Falls Bridge…attached to a bungee cord.

"Now *that* would make a memory, Dad!" Aaron pleaded.

"The truth is, I won't even get a scratch. And I have the money!"

I'm not sure what I would have done, but Peter agreed—after a careful inspection of the equipment and reassurances from the operators that the cord wouldn't break even if Aaron were an elephant. Aaron paid his money, got strapped in, and hurled himself headfirst off the bridge.

Aaron screamed. Peter nearly had a heart attack. But the cord held. And Aaron had so much fun that he took a second jump.

Do you trust God enough to let the truth change the way you think and act? When Jabez prayed to the God of Israel, he was wholeheartedly casting his future on the simple truth of God's extravagant goodness. And God gave him a huge, new life.

I'm not asking you to be foolish, just outrageously, joyously confident in your God. He wants you to know the truth about His plans for you today: *My plans for you are only good. What I want for you is greater than anything you've seen so far. And you can trust Me completely!*

My Jabez Journal: *If I trusted God completely for my future, what risks could I take for Him today?*

Faith expects from God what is beyond all expectation.

Andrew Murray

Week Three

"O Lord, Put Your Hand upon Me!"

God's work done in God's way
will never lack God's supply.

Hudson Taylor

HE PROVIDES *the* POWER

For our gospel did not come to you in word only, but also in power, and in the Holy Spirit and in much assurance.

1 THESSALONIANS 1:5

Very soon after you step out to live on a larger scale for God, you will realize that overwhelming new obstacles are mushrooming right along with your grand new opportunities…only you have remained as small and weak as ever.

Not a happy moment, humanly speaking, but an enormously promising one spiritually.

It is natural to feel overwhelmed when we see the outrageous predicament (that's Jabez talk for "God-given opportunity") that our bold praying has gotten us into. We're struck by the limits of our powers and the certainty of our failure. We feel like we're on the *Titanic* bailing water with a paper cup. Who wouldn't feel a touch of despair?

Yet that's one reason God often asks us to challenge daunting odds—He wants to grow the size of our faith to match the size of His destiny for us. And it's during these awakenings to our great need that we're driven to cry out, "O Lord, put Your hand on me!"

At these moments of our own powerlessness, we're finally ready to be vessels for God's power.

Jabez understood this: He received the blessing, took on greater territories, and quickly became aware that without power from on high, he had fatally overstepped his bounds. But instead of turning back or praying for fewer problems, he prayed for *more* power.

In the Bible, the hand (or arm) of the Lord stands for God's power and presence. For example:

- "The hand of God was on Judah to give them singleness of heart to obey the command of the king" (2 Chronicles 30:12).
- "Behold, the LORD's hand is not shortened, that it cannot save" (Isaiah 59:1).
- "Ah, Lord GOD! Behold, You have made the heavens and the earth by Your great power and outstretched arm. There is nothing too hard for You" (Jeremiah 32:17).

In the New Testament, "the hand of the Lord" is given credit for the amazing spread of the gospel after Pentecost (Acts 11:21). The more common New Testament synonym for God's hand is the filling of the Holy Spirit. Just before He ascended, Jesus said, "You shall receive power when the Holy Spirit has come upon you; and you shall be witnesses to Me" (Acts 1:8).

Have you ever tried to take territory for God—even speak for Him—and suddenly realized that you were not up to the task? I can't tell you how many times I've thrown my hands up and told God, "No! It can't be done!" And I can't tell you how many times

God has had the last word in that dispute.

A few years ago as part of our WorldTeach ministry, I was praying for a miraculous increase in Bible teachers across the world. The goal was steep—too steep for comfort. And if we failed, what would that say about our vision? How would we find the faith to take on next year's goal? December 31 came, and we were several teachers short. Devastated, I poured out a prayer to God.

Several days later, my associate came rushing into my office. A country had just reported in with amended numbers, and the new tally showed that we had actually met our goal...*and surpassed it.*

That was God leaving His calling card. He wanted us to know who carried the power in this project. And He wanted our faith to grow to meet the size of our opportunity.

If you feel in over your head right now, then this is your week to experience God's power in new ways.

What overwhelms you today? What is the goal you feel incapable of completing? Draw a small picture or symbol of it in a box. Write its name inside the box too. Then draw a wide circle around your box to represent God. He is greater; He surrounds your challenge. In that box, put words and symbols for other challenges you face as well. Then pray over your drawing until you accept in your deepest heart that God is *bigger* than any opportunity or any obstacle.

On your Jabez journey, you can expect moments of weakness. But remember that even in the midst of your need, your faith muscles are being stretched. You're building a deeper trust. And God is at work. If you're taking on His purposes, He will provide the power.

My Jabez Journal: *In all my life, when have I most seen God's power at work through me?*

Do not pray for tasks equal to your powers.
Pray for powers equal to your tasks.

Phillips Brooks

And the Lord said to Moses, "Has the Lord's arm been shortened?
Now you shall see whether what I say will happen to you or not."

Numbers 11:23

"By My Spirit"

"This is the word of the Lord to Zerubbabel: 'Not by might nor by power, but by My Spirit,' says the Lord of hosts."
Zechariah 4:6

In late nineteenth-century England, Charles Spurgeon was by all accounts the greatest preacher in the capital of the most powerful nation on earth. Huge throngs, including the wealthy and powerful, came to London's cavernous Metropolitan Tabernacle to hear him preach the gospel.

But my favorite Spurgeon story is his own account of his *worst* sermon.

Spurgeon held himself to towering standards, always fearing his best wasn't good enough. One day, his worst fears were realized when he preached an awful sermon. He was so traumatized by his poor work that he rushed home and fell to his knees. "O Lord, I'm so feeble and You're so powerful!" he prayed. "Only You can make something of such a ghastly sermon. Please use it and bless it."

You or I might have told him to put his failure behind him and move on, but Spurgeon kept praying all week for God to use the terrible sermon. Meanwhile, he set about to do better the following Sunday. And he did. At the conclusion of that sermon, the audience of thousands all but carried him out on their shoulders.

But Spurgeon was not to be fooled. He decided to keep careful records of the results of the two sermons. Within a few months the outcome was clear. The "ghastly" sermon had led forty-one people to know Christ; his masterpiece had led to no observable results at all.

Spurgeon knew or suspected what most forget: Our success in ministry is never about ability in the first place, but about God's power and our dependence on it. Spurgeon leaned on God in his weakness, and God blessed his flawed efforts.

As you make yourself more and more available for God's purposes, you will be asked to accomplish more and more. Of course, nothing takes the place of responsible preparation for the task at hand—God isn't in the business of compensating for laziness or lack of commitment. But at every step, the true purpose of eternity is accomplished by His Spirit, not yours. All you offer is the vessel. You must be filled up for service.

Like Jabez, Zerubbabel is another little-known Bible person who faced an impossible task. The pain in his life was a national one—he led the first group of Jews that returned from captivity to find their homeland overrun by foreigners and their temple in ruins. But Zerubbabel's pain was personal too—he was a direct descendant of King David (1 Chronicles 3:1–19) and could have been heir to the throne...but there was no throne.

In these difficult circumstances, God asked Zerubbabel to rebuild the temple. The task seemed impossible. The Jews were demoralized and poor, and opposition by pagan outsiders to a new temple was intense. But through the prophet Zechariah, God encouraged Zerubbabel with a memorable message: "This is the word of the LORD to Zerubbabel: 'Not by might nor by power, but by My Spirit,' says the LORD of hosts" (Zechariah 4:6).

In the same message, God promised that Zerubbabel would be able to finish the temple, and He gave his servant a picture of how his success would come: "'Who are you, O great mountain? Before Zerubbabel you shall become a plain!'" (Zechariah 4:7).

Do you see the amazing sequence of Zerubbabel's commissioning?

1. *God gave* this "Jabez" a mountain to move.
2. *God told* him that he would fail to move the mountain on his own.
3. *God promised* to move the mountain for him.

If you're facing a mountain today, *there's a good chance that you're in the right place*—a place where God's supernatural power can be released for His glory. If you're keenly aware of a recent "ghastly" attempt to speak for God, ask God to continue to fill up your inadequate effort with His incomparable power.

The greatness of your need may finally be giving God room to move.

My Jabez Journal: *Trace the evidences of God's power as recorded in Isaiah 40:10–31. Where in my life am I doubting this ability to be powerful on my behalf today?*

"But also if you say to this mountain, 'Be removed and be cast into the sea,' it will be done. And whatever things you ask in prayer, believing, you will receive."

Matthew 21:21–22

You never become truly spiritual by sitting down and wishing to become so. You must undertake something so great that you cannot accomplish it unaided.

Phillips Brooks

THE BOTTOMLESS BASKET

"Behold, I am the LORD, the God of all flesh.
Is there anything too hard for Me?"
JEREMIAH 32:27

A restaurant put up a sign that said, All You Can Eat for $4.99. A hungry man came in, paid his $4.99, and polished off a huge helping. Then he ordered more and finished that too. But when he put in his order for a third meal, the waitress turned him down. The man angrily called for the manager and pointed to the sign in the window. "It says, All You Can Eat for $4.99, and I can still eat more!" he complained.

The manager stood his ground. "Yes, but *I'm* the guy who says that's *all you can eat for $4.99!"*

Do you suspect that God might be like that manager? As good as His word, but only up to a point?

At each step of your journey into the Jabez adventure, you will have to face your own deeply rooted suspicions about God. Everyone does. Somehow we have to face and "unlearn" old ways of thinking:

- that God only wants to bless me a little bit;

• that while God may have a plan for me, it's probably not very important;

• that God's power is only rarely available, at least for little old me!

You see, we put God in a box. Inside that box, He can be God. But outside the box, we let our skepticism, fear, and meager expectations rule.

So much of Christ's ministry on earth was a direct assault on this tyranny of "God in a Box." Look, for example, at another all-you-can-eat story: the feeding of the five thousand in the New Testament. This event is so important that it is the only miracle apart from the Resurrection to be recorded in all four Gospels. (Another feeding of four thousand is also told in Matthew and Mark.)

The account in John 6 shows a logistical nightmare that would make any seasoned event planner cringe. Crowds of ill-prepared people have followed Jesus up into the hills. By the end of the day, they are hungry and far from home, and night is approaching. Every sign points to catastrophe. I'm sure the disciples figured that by morning, Jesus' "career" would be straggling home along with His last cold and starving followers. Yet starting with a boy's lunch, Jesus feeds the crowd, leaving everyone satisfied and with food to spare.

But don't miss how the disciples felt before God moved. Their concerns were valid. Their doubts were real. Their situation was genuinely desperate. That point of need before God moves is where you will be tested again and again if you choose to live with God's hand upon you.

It doesn't matter whether you are short of money, people, energy, or time. What God invites you to do will always be greater than the resources you start with. Living with the hand of God upon you means that at times you'll be asked to act in spite of the evidence…and then watch the evidence change.

Ask God to show you today any old ways of thinking—wrong assumptions about how success happens or how God works. Then let your God be who He really is. He is a God of power—available, essential, and unlimited—and there is no box.

My Jabez Journal: *"Lord, show me how I have limited Your power by my ignorance or unbelief. I want You to be God in my life."*

When you have nothing left but God, then
for the first time you become aware that God is enough.

Maude Royden

Power *with* Purpose

"But you shall receive power when the Holy Spirit has come upon you; and you shall be witnesses to Me in Jerusalem, and in all Judea and Samaria, and to the end of the earth."

Acts 1:8

Russell, a friend of mine, was sixteen when he first became serious about his faith. He still remembers his first experience of stepping out in weakness and experiencing God's strength. After a youth group concert one afternoon in a shopping center parking lot, a woman walked up and began questioning Russell about his faith. Although he had never had to give a defense of his faith before, Russell found himself engaging easily with the woman.

Afterward, Russell recalls, the kids gathered around in astonishment. They wanted to know where he'd learned to speak like an international ambassador. But Russell was as surprised as them. "It was as if someone else jumped in and began speaking for me," he remembers.

When I ask audiences about similar experiences, I hear two recurring themes: "I was scared to death" and "When it was all over, I realized that God spoke through me to that person."

Friend, letting the Spirit speak through us is meant to happen on a regular basis. This is the *normal* Christian life. You and I are called to be His ambassadors—He rarely uses any other option. He's not going to speak from heaven at our workplace or in school hallways. He won't send an e-mail to your straying friend. God needs the mouths of His people to be filled with His Spirit.

Jesus told His disciples in Luke 12:11–12 that the Holy Spirit would give them the words to say in their hour of need. He repeats the same promise later:

> *"You will be brought before kings and rulers for My name's sake. But it will turn out for you as an occasion for testimony. Therefore settle it in your hearts not to meditate beforehand on what you will answer; for I will give you...wisdom which all your adversaries will not be able to contradict or resist." (Luke 21:12–15)*

If you want to see this promise in action, there's no better reading than the book of Acts. Here, you watch Peter, John, Stephen, and Paul testify fearlessly and effectively for Christ—and you see the Holy Spirit bring in the harvest.

In Acts 1:8, Jesus offered the simplest definition of the Spirit's purpose: "But you shall receive power when the Holy Spirit has come upon you; and *you shall be witnesses to Me.*"

Think of the filling of the Holy Spirit as electrical power: You have electricity wired into your home for many purposes. You use it as needed. If you use some, more is available. Spiritual power is similar. When you're ready to enlarge your territory, the Spirit of God will increase the power flow within you. You'll *know* you're working in the realm of a power greater than yourself. And though you'll be changed by that kind of experience, you'll need to stay connected to the source of power to keep getting results.

The New Testament uses the word picture of "filling" as if the Spirit were a fluid, and you need to come back often for a refill. When Paul urges, "Be filled with the Spirit" (Ephesians 5:18), he literally means to *go on being filled* with the Spirit. This kind of filling is different from the permanent residence of God's Spirit in you at the time of your salvation. But He does fill you more for specific ministry tasks...if you ask.

Acts records three separate incidents when Peter was filled with the Holy Spirit. Ask God to fill you mightily with the Spirit every day. You are not asking for a feeling or to enter some special zone; you are asking for God's power. You are not asking for outrageous behavior; the Holy Spirit does everything peaceably and in order (1 Corinthians 14:33). You are not asking to lose control; the Spirit doesn't want to take away your thoughts or overrule your personality. You are asking for God to work *through* you and to work through you mightily.

Has it been a while since you put your mouth on the line for God? Here's a promise for you to take with you today: "I am the LORD your God...open your mouth wide, and I will fill it" (Psalm 81:10).

MY JABEZ JOURNAL: *When was the last time I prayed specifically and urgently to be filled with the Holy Spirit?*

There is not one single passage in the Old Testament or the New Testament where the filling with the Holy Spirit is spoken of and not connected with the testimony of service.

R. A. TORREY

Now hope does not disappoint, because the love of God has been poured out in our hearts by the Holy Spirit who was given to us.

ROMANS 5:5

The Brave *and the* Bold

For God has not given us a spirit of fear, but of power and of love and of a sound mind.

2 Timothy 1:7

The famous nineteenth-century preacher Henry Ward Beecher once took on the forces of corruption in his city of Indianapolis. He did more than identify the sins—he named the sinners, calling on the leaders of the liquor and gambling industries to repent.

One night, as Beecher was walking through the city, one of these unsavory characters stepped out of an alley and pointed a gun at him. "Retract what you said, Reverend, or I'll fire," he growled.

"Fire away," Beecher said, and kept walking. "I don't believe you can hit the mark as well as I did." The assailant put down his gun.

You have to admire Beecher's boldness. The courage to oppose popular points of view or stand up for moral absolutes is especially difficult in these days when our culture worships comfort, tolerance, and protecting personal choice. Yet courage has been called the cornerstone of the virtues. When we lose it, we become incapable of any other virtue.

The best way I know to live boldly is to live in the power of the Spirit. Yesterday I suggested that you look through the book of Acts to get a good picture of how the power of the Holy Spirit surges through us when we step up to do God's work. You see the word *boldness* three times just in Acts 4. It's not too surprising because Christians were spreading the gospel in hostile environments—synagogues, jails, rock-throwing mobs, Roman courts, even among dissenting fellow believers.

But you might say, "I'm no Paul, and I'm no Reverend Beecher, either. Can I still be courageous—even bold—for God?"

Yes. Meet a wallflower named Timothy, a junior pastor whom Paul calls his "true son in the faith" (1 Timothy 1:2). The two men could hardly have been more different. Paul was fearless; Timothy was bashful. Paul was decisive; Timothy fretted. Paul loved to improvise; Timothy preferred order and routine. When necessary, Paul didn't hesitate to be confrontational; Timothy took great risks to keep the peace.

Yet Paul saw in his young protégé a prince for God. You catch the flavor of Paul's affection and vision for Timothy in this familiar passage:

> *To Timothy, a beloved son.... I remind you to stir up the gift of God which is in you through the laying on of my hands.* For God has not given us a spirit of fear, but of power and of love and of a sound mind. *Therefore do not be ashamed of the testimony*

of our Lord, nor of me His prisoner, but share with me in the sufferings for the gospel according to the power of God" (2 Timothy 1:2, 6–8, emphasis mine).

Did Timothy allow his retiring nature to hinder God's destiny for him? Not at all. He became the leader of the believers at Ephesus, probably the largest church of that era. In Paul's last letter from prison, he commends Timothy as "like-minded" (Philippians 2:20) and sincerely caring: "You know his proven character, that as a son with his father he served with me in the gospel" (v. 22).

Do you have moments of fear when you face the great task God has set before you? That's normal. Be assured that, at the right time, God will provide you with the right words to say and a boldness to say them that you never thought possible.

My Jabez Journal: *What specific fear is keeping me from being bold for God? What is the worst thing that could happen if that fear proved true? What good thing could happen?*

Give me a hundred men who fear nothing but sin, and desire nothing but God, and I will shake the world. I care not a straw whether they be clergymen or laymen; and such alone will overthrow the kingdom of Satan and build up the Kingdom of God on earth.

JOHN WESLEY

And when they had prayed, the place where they were assembled together was shaken; and they were all filled with the Holy Spirit, and they spoke the word of God with boldness.

ACTS 4:31

NO PRIDE INSIDE

Now when the multitudes saw it, they marveled and glorified God, who had given such power to men.

MATTHEW 9:8

Handel's *Messiah* glorifies the name of God more powerfully than any music I've heard. Its climax, the "Hallelujah Chorus," never fails to stir my emotions. The composer consciously committed his work to God's glory, and God has used it for more than a quarter of a millennium. But have you heard the story of its first performance?

On March 23, 1743, Handel premiered his oratorio in London to an audience that included the king. As the piece progressed, everyone seemed to know they were beholding something timeless and holy. When the "Hallelujah Chorus" opened, the king was so overcome by emotion that he sprang to his feet. Out of protocol, the rest of the crowd rose too. Along with the king, everyone remained standing until the final strains of the music echoed through the hall. Ever since, whenever the chorus is performed, audiences rise. "King of kings!" sings the choir. "Lord of lords! And He shall reign forever and ever!"

Bringing God that much glory for all eternity is the great goal of the Jabez life. Yet the easiest slip to make when we see God working powerfully through us is to take the credit for ourselves. But God does not want to share His glory, even with you and me, His chosen children—He wants all of it (Isaiah 42:8). Listen to this amazing declaration about Himself that God makes to Moses: "You shall worship no other god, for the LORD, whose name is Jealous, is a jealous God" (Exodus 34:14). And remember, the first four of the Ten Commandments focus on protecting God's name and honor and glory.

Most Christians struggle with this issue of personal glorification. How difficult it is to be in the spotlight yet focus the spotlight on someone else! And the more you and I are part of great things for God, the more tempting it becomes to believe that we are somehow the cause of, and necessary to, those great things.

But usurping the glory of God is a serious offense. You could ask Moses about that. He took his eyes off God while doing God's work—bringing water from a stone—and was therefore disobedient. Improvising on God's clear instructions, Moses stole glory that belonged to God; the demonstration was now about Moses instead of God and His exceeding power. As a consequence of taking God's glory, Moses was never allowed to enter the Promised Land (Numbers 20:12). The glory is God's and God's alone, and the purpose of the Spirit is always to magnify His name.

We all need to hear words of encouragement, but there is a line where how we receive praise moves from being spiritually nourishing to being pridefully self-serving. Think over the last few days, and ask God to point out times when you've coveted glory in some way. I encourage you to note them in your journal. "God forbid that I should boast except in the cross of our Lord Jesus Christ," wrote Paul, "by whom the world has been crucified to me, and I to the world" (Galatians 6:14).

May I tell you about one more great composer? His name was Haydn, and he composed a masterwork, taken from Scripture, called *The Creation.* One year before his death, he was just healthy enough to hear it performed. As they rolled him into the auditorium in a wheelchair, pandemonium broke out. Applause and calls of praise rained down on the great musician. It took all of Haydn's strength to pull himself to his feet, raise his hands toward heaven, and shout, "No, No! Not from me, but from *there*—from heaven above comes all!"

His old, crackling voice must have been music to God's ears.

MY JABEZ JOURNAL: *What person in my life inspires me the most by how he or she brings glory to God?*

As long as we take glory from one another, as long as ever we seek and love and jealously guard the glory of this life—the honor and reputation that comes from men—we do not seek and cannot receive the glory that comes from God. Pride renders faith impossible.

ANDREW MURRAY

RIGHT HERE, RIGHT NOW

Behold, now is the accepted time; behold, now is the day of salvation.

2 CORINTHIANS 6:2

The couple in flowered shirts sharing the elevator with me looked middle-aged and just a little bored. I had just arrived to lead a seminar on spiritual breakthroughs. As it turned out, they would be attending my seminar.

"So what kind of breakthrough do you folks want?" I asked.

The husband said their marriage had been in a terrible state for some time. In fact, he said they weren't sure it was worth saving, but they were hoping for some kind of breakthrough soon.

"Do you want to salvage your marriage?" I asked.

They said "Of course!" together.

"Does God want you to salvage it?" I asked. They both said yes.

"Then there's no 'soon' about this! God wants you to have that breakthrough in your marriage *right now.*"

"You mean right here in this elevator?" the man asked with a nervous laugh.

I was ready with my yes when we arrived at their floor. We

stepped out into a little lobby. As we stood there together looking over the city, we talked about the actions and events that had so deeply injured their relationship. "Do you believe God's power is fully available to you right here by this window?" I asked. When they nodded, we prayed together.

As we parted, I gave them a few starting points for renewing their relationship. I said, "You can trust God to begin rebuilding your marriage immediately, you know." Again, they both seemed shocked. I told them to keep me posted on how they were doing during the course of the next two days.

God saved that marriage, I'm happy to tell you. And it happened because of a strong spiritual principle: *God's power is given for the here and now.* We may think and deliberate and mull things over for months, but God is ready to begin immediately when it comes to matters of His will.

Think about the implications:

- If God is asking you to stop an activity that is compromising your life or dishonoring Him, His power to help you do it is available right now. His will is that you do it *now.*
- If you need to get your finances in shape or bring your stewardship habits in line, His wisdom and power are at your disposal at a moment's notice. And His will is that you do it *now.*
- If your friend needs to hear the message of salvation, the Holy Spirit is ready now to help you take the first step and say the first sentence. And His will is that you do it *now.*

In Acts 8, Philip shared the gospel with a traveler from Ethiopia who was so excited that he said, "See, here is water. What hinders me from being baptized?" (v. 36). The answer? Nothing at all! Why wait? Philip didn't. And as soon as that salvation breakthrough was complete, "the Spirit of the Lord caught Philip away" on another important mission (v. 39).

That phrase—"caught away"—captures the eagerness and urgency God feels for you and me to bring the Good News to the whole world:

- What hinders you from being God's spokesman in your own home?
- What hinders you from being fruitful for God on the job?
- A world of need surrounds you. What hinders you from manifesting God's power and enlarging the population of heaven?

No time to wait. No "business as usual." You can serve Him right here, right now—and then the Spirit of God will catch you away to some new and significant task for Him.

Don't you want to live out that kind of adventure? Can you think of anything more worthy of your entire devotion? God's power and presence are ready for you... *right now.*

My Jabez Journal: *What new thing is God asking me to do today?*

*I resolve to live with all my might while I do live.
I resolve never to lose one moment of time
and to improve my use of time in the most
profitable way I possibly can. I resolve never to do
anything I wouldn't do if it were the last hour of my life.*

JONATHAN EDWARDS

Week Four

"O Lord, Keep Me from Evil!"

Many are they who say of me, "There is no help for him in God." But You, O Lord, are a shield for me, my glory and the one who lifts up my head.

Psalm 3:2–3

Don't Even Go There!

"Do not lead us into temptation, but deliver us from the evil one."

Matthew 6:13

When you take territory for God, you are taking it from someone else. You are fighting against sin—in yourself, in the world, and in the spiritual realm. If you've never experienced true opposition before, you will now.

That's why Jabez's plea to be kept from evil is so necessary and even revolutionary.

Have you noticed that this part of the Jabez prayer parallels the prayer that Jesus taught His disciples? When the disciples asked, "Lord, teach us to pray" (Luke 11:1), Jesus gave His friends a model prayer. One of its three requests had to do with temptation (the other two were for provision and forgiveness). He said, "When you pray, say:...do not lead us into temptation, but deliver us from the evil one" (vv. 2, 4).

From this we learn that the most important strategy for beating temptation is to avoid it altogether. In the coming week, we're going to look at some important ways we can strive to live a sin-free life. But Jabez would remind us today that the first tactic is also the best: *Stay out of the contest. Don't even go near it!*

Does the simple truth of this advice shock you? It should. It runs against our prideful, risk-loving reflexes. We *like* to play with danger, to have options, and to take trouble head-on, believing we can always pack on more power than our opponents.

But with temptation, these instincts get us in trouble. Why? First, temptation pits you against your own sin nature and all the powers of evil. That combination can lead you to sin. And God doesn't want you to sin. Sin weakens you and compromises your ability to receive God's favor and power.

Second, if you were never tempted, you would never sin. Why would you? That's why Satan initiated his deceptive encounter in the Garden. He was creating what the Bible calls "an occasion to sin." We need to stay away from the occasion whenever possible. As someone has said, "He who would not eat forbidden fruit must stay away from the forbidden tree." Therefore, when your first line of defense is to pray "Keep me away from evil" compared to "Keep me from sinning," you've made a huge leap toward victory.

If you think I'm splitting meanings like hairs, you need to talk to someone who has overcome drunkenness. They'll tell you that *having decided not to drink,* they stay out of bars, out of liquor stores, and away from drinking friends. They don't keep alcohol in the house, and they don't put "happy hour" as an option on their schedule. They have simply chosen *in advance* to lose some pleasures in order to gain other, infinitely more valuable ones.

On day an acquaintance confided to me that he was struggling with pornography. Some time ago, he said, he had started pulling into an adult video store on his way home from work. Now it had become a habit.

"Is there another route you can take to get home?" I asked. By the look on his face, I could tell he'd never considered that option. He thought a while, then continued. "But when I get home I watch trashy shows on HBO after my wife is asleep."

"Do you really want to quit?" I asked. He said yes.

"Then cancel your HBO subscription."

"Oh, I don't know if I can do *that!*" he exclaimed.

"Well," I replied, "at least when you're ready, you'll know exactly what to do so you'll never have to fall into that sin again." A few weeks later, he called me to say he was driving a different way home, his HBO subscription was history, and he was enjoying sleeping next to his wife in peace.

It's a refreshing thought, isn't it, that you and I can ask God to help us avoid evil? Like a father near a rapids who warns his child, "Honey, don't even go out on those rocks!" God is watching out for you. If you ask Him, He'll tell you where *not* to go.

Your part is to pray for protection from evil today, to thank Him for His care, and to obey.

My Jabez Journal: *When have I sensed the Spirit warning me away from an arena of temptation? What happened?*

"Watch and pray, lest you enter into temptation.
The spirit indeed is willing, but the flesh is weak."

Matthew 26:41

Better shun the bait than struggle in the snare.

John Dryden

FINDING *the* ESCAPE HATCH

No temptation has overtaken you except such as is common to man; but God is faithful, who will not allow you to be tempted beyond what you are able, but with the temptation will also make the way of escape, that you may be able to bear it.

1 CORINTHIANS 10:13

Imagine for a minute that you are standing in front of your home. You see a stranger coming up your street. He's dressed all in black, and as he walks in your direction, you notice that he's checking mailboxes and house numbers. You realize that this figure is here to do you harm, so you duck behind some bushes. As soon as the stranger finds your address, he steps up to your door and knocks.

As you watch, the door opens, and you see something remarkable. The person answering the door is Jesus.

The stranger hesitates. "Excuse me, but isn't this the home of _____?" And he speaks your name.

Jesus replies, "As a matter of fact, it is. But My friend has asked Me to guard the door."

The stranger tenses, grinds his teeth, and seems to consider forcing his way in. Then he looks down at the hand on the knob.

He sees the nail scars. He glances up at Jesus' head and the marks left by the thorns.

And the stranger scowls as he turns away....

I've described a defensive strategy used by Martin Luther, the great reformer of the sixteenth century, when he faced temptations of all kinds. On the front lines of a spiritual awakening that was shaking the world, Luther felt himself under constant attack. His story of Jesus answering the door of his home when temptations came calling had a specific purpose. It was his way of meditating on a powerful truth about Christ's power to help us escape temptation: "For in that He Himself has suffered, being tempted, He is able to aid those who are tempted" (Hebrews 2:18).

Did you notice the wonderful "escape clause" in today's verse? In His faithfulness, God pledges to not allow any temptation to push you beyond your ability to resist. Because "with the temptation" will be provided "*the* way of escape" (1 Corinthians 10:13). Note that the Bible doesn't say "*a* way."

Here's how I put that truth to work in my life. If I'm really tempted to sin, I say aloud: "This temptation to [name the sin] is *not* too strong for me, because my Father has limited it to what I'm able to cope with right this minute!"

Then I add: "And the truth of it is, there is a way out of this temptation right this very minute, and God will not allow it to overpower me."

I can assure you that temptations don't like to be caught in the glare of that much truth! When you bring them out into the open by speaking their name and standing on His promises, they run back into the dark, whimpering. Then you see these allurements for what they really are—puny, pathetic devices sent to obstruct and damage.

Do you understand now that God will help you in temptation? More than help you—protect you from being tempted beyond your strength to resist? More than protect you—*open the way for you to escape?*

It's all true! You won't need to be afraid again, but then, neither will you be able to make excuses again. Jesus Christ has already faced this temptation for you. And He has already made your way of escape.

MY JABEZ JOURNAL: *In what challenging circumstances have I been most successful at avoiding temptation? What principles can I identify from these experiences that I could apply in areas where I'm still struggling?*

The Lord knows how to deliver the godly out of temptations.

2 PETER 2:9

Decoding Defeat

Each one is tempted when he is drawn away by his own desires and enticed.

James 1:14

What if you could walk into the tent of the enemy's general today and overhear his plan for rolling over your defenses? Wouldn't you go about your day in a whole different way, adjusting your moves to counter his, much more confident about your prospects for winning?

I want to help you do that. Satan knows that you'll never be able to break free from your cycles of sin until you open your eyes to your behavior patterns and take a hard look at the persistent appeal of the sin itself. That's why if you look closely at your defeats, you'll recognize your enemy's favorite strategies to do you in.

When I lead groups on the subject of personal holiness, I ask participants to make an inventory of the one or two recurring sins that trouble them most. You see, even though you're capable of many different sins, your main struggle with temptation usually comes down to two or three behaviors that you repeat on a regular basis, often for years. One of the ways you flee temptation, then, is to uncover these patterns and respond with a plan for success.

The following questions can help you create a personal sin profile:

1. *On what day of the week do I sin most?*
2. *At what time of day do I sin most?*
3. *Where am I when I sin most?*
4. *Who is with me when I sin most?*
5. *What sin or sins do I commit the most in these circumstances?*

Take a moment to make your own replies. By the way, I've found that 80 percent of respondents create the same profile: "I sin the most on Friday or Saturday, in the evening, at home, when I'm alone."

Now I want you to think a little harder:

6. *What are the specific, negative emotions that I feel right before I sin?* Turn your answer into a personal finding: "The negative emotions I feel right before I give in to temptation are ___________."

Most are startled to discover that the feelings they record show a recurring pattern—the same feelings leading to the same failures in a repeating cycle. Participants most commonly list feeling overwhelmed, lonely, rejected, bored, betrayed, worthless, weary, angry, or anxious—anything but peace and comfort.

Now you're ready for the final question:

7. *At the point of my temptation, what does the sinful behavior promise me?* Most people reply: "The promise of the temptation is that if I commit that sin, the negative feeling I'm experiencing at the time will go away or be replaced by a strong, positive one."

Whether we're trying to seek pleasure or escape pain, the power of temptation comes from its promise: "I can make you feel better right now." Of course, God made us to dislike pain and enjoy pleasure. There's no sin in that. The damage comes when we look for the right thing in the wrong place.

So ask God to help you decide what you can do now to prepare for—*avoid, compensate for, prevent the occurrence of*—those recurring negative feelings that set you up for a fall. Then when you see the enemy lining up the same old plan today to squash you, you'll have a positive alternative in place.

Do you want to escape? I hope so!

> *Do not, then, allow sin to establish any power over your mortal bodies in making you give way to its lusts.... But, like men rescued from certain death, put yourselves in God's hands as weapons of good for His own purposes. For sin can never be your master. (Romans 6:12–14, Phillips)*

My Jabez Journal: *What pleasure is leading me into sin lately? What pain? Are they connected?*

If you keep doing what you've always done,
you'll always get what you've always gotten.

John Maxwell

Temptation rarely comes in working hours.
It is in their leisure time that men are made or marred.

W. N. Taylor

THE THREE-MINUTE TEMPTATION BUSTER

Now the Lord is the Spirit; and where the Spirit of the Lord is, there is liberty.

2 CORINTHIANS 3:17

Yesterday we looked at patterns of sin—those recurring responses to temptation that account for the largest part of the "sin problem" in our lives. Today I want to help you make a breakthrough that begins with what we've learned, and asks a further question: "Whether I sin to get pleasure or to mask pain, wouldn't I be less likely to sin if I found myself no longer distressed but comforted?"

Years ago, I found myself so wanting *not* to sin in a particular area yet continually beseiged by temptation. Was there no real answer for victory, I wondered? I still remember exactly where I was sitting when the Lord opened my understanding to an obvious, but little-understood, answer that has helped me and thousand of others.

Here's what happened: After I realized that I was distressed right before every temptation and that I was ultimately seeking comfort, I asked God to show me another way to find it. That's when I remembered Jesus' promise to send comfort.

> *And I will pray the Father, and he shall give you another Comforter, that he may abide with you for ever; Even the Spirit of truth; whom the world cannot receive, because it seeth him not, neither knoweth him; but ye know him, for he dwelleth with you, and shall be in you.* (John 14:16–17, KJV)

Incredibly, Jesus gave us the Holy Spirit to be our indwelling, personal source of comfort. Somehow, I'd never linked this supernatural provision to my struggle with sin. I wondered what would happen if I specifically asked for this divine comfort in a time of temptation. Would the Holy Spirit give to me the needed comfort so that I would feel less need to sin?

I decided to try. "Dear Holy Spirit," I prayed, "You've been sent to me to be my personal Comforter. I am in desperate need of comfort. I don't want to sin. Please comfort me. In Jesus' name. Amen."

I took off my watch to see what would happen. At first, nothing did. But at some point I became aware that I did feel comfort. I didn't know exactly when the comfort had happened, only that it had. My soul felt soothed and no longer in pain.

When I turned back toward that temptation, I found that it had already receded into the darkness, far from my senses. I was free. Instead of finding it hard not to sin, I now found it easy because the pull of that sin had faded, and my deepest need had been met.

I've prayed to my Comforter many times since then, and I've discovered two truths. First, the Holy Spirit always—and I mean always—completes His responsibility in my heart. Second—and this may surprise you—He always gives me His comfort within three minutes, though I can never put my finger on the exact second when He does it.

Now I call this prayer for comfort the Three-Minute Temptation Buster. When you feel sorely tempted to sin today, remember that you can take your underlying need for fulfillment and comfort to God. Ask for His Comforter to comfort you. Then take off your watch and time this miracle of God's intervention—I can guarantee that the Spirit will comfort you in less than three minutes. And by then you won't need to sin because the temptation will have vanished.

My Jabez Journal: *Have I ever asked for the comfort the Holy Spirit brings? When have I experienced it lately?*

Walk in the Spirit, and you shall not fulfill the lust of the flesh....
The fruit of the Spirit is love, joy, peace,
longsuffering, kindness, goodness, faithfulness, gentleness, self-control.

Galatians 5:16, 22–23

OPPOSING FORCES

Be sober, be vigilant; because your adversary the devil walks about like a roaring lion, seeking whom he may devour. Resist him, steadfast in faith.

1 PETER 5:8–9

During Bible times, wild lions still roamed the thickets along the Jordan and in the desolate areas of the region's deserts and mountains. So to describe Satan as a hungry lion stalking its prey was a vivid picture for early Christians. Some commentators think this reference in 1 Peter may have held a double meaning for them: It also described how Emperor Nero singled out Christians to be sent to die in arenas full of ravenous beasts.

Have you "heard" your spiritual adversary roaring on the fringes of your life lately, perhaps even snapping his jaws in your face?

Our adversary is real. He is a spiritual being who instigates persecution and suffering, and his aim is to destroy our faith. Yet we don't need to live in fear of him. Interestingly, our defense against spiritual attack is supposed to be different than against temptation. As we've seen, we're advised to "flee" temptations (2 Timothy 2:22). But we're told, *"Resist* the devil and he will flee from you" (James 4:7, emphasis mine).

The ones who attract Satan's attention are the ones who are serious about actually doing something for God. You can recognize his oppression by some telltale signs:

- Everything you do connected with God's work will become much harder than it should be, and for no other explainable reason.
- You'll be filled with emotional turmoil: You'll feel overwhelmed, unworthy, confused, distracted, and full of doubt; you'll want to quit; you'll feel like you're the wrong person for the job; you may even find yourself saying, "I'd rather just die."

Friend, these are Satan's standard operating procedures. All believers who want to serve God in a significant way will face opposition of this kind, especially when we sign up to accomplish more for God, and it's all with one end in mind—to make us quit.

Every spiritual advance we read about in the Bible is opposed by the enemy in these same ways. One of best case studies is found in the book of Nehemiah. Nehemiah has taken up the challenge to help the returning exiles rebuild the wall around Jerusalem. Without a city wall, Jerusalem is defenseless against marauders, and God's people must live in disgrace (Nehemiah 2:17).

In the first six chapters of the book, Nehemiah's mission for God and country is opposed by ridicule (2:19), resistance (3:5), discouragement within the ranks (4:10), threats of violence (4:11), false accusations (6:5–9), and corruption (6:17–19).

But Nehemiah resists. He counterattacks with constant prayer and an unswerving trust in God's calling and favor. He leads by example—encouraging, exhorting, problem-solving at every turn. When the opposition threatens to attack, Nehemiah assigns all his men to carry weapons; half build at a time while the other half stand guard. "So we continued the work," he reports, "with half the men holding spears, from the first light of dawn till the stars came out" (4:21, NIV).

After months of this kind of diligence, Nehemiah and his builders succeed. The wall is finished. Nehemiah has "taken back" Jerusalem from the ruins and brought glory to God.

To continue taking territory for God today, start with Peter's advice to be "sober and vigilant." Recording your victories and struggles in your Jabez journal is a powerful tool for doing just that. Soberness comes from knowing the facts about your ravenous spiritual opponents and drawing around yourself the supreme protection and favor of God and the full armor available for spiritual warfare (Ephesians 6:11, 13).

Vigilance will keep you alert for his roar and safe from his jaws.

MY JABEZ JOURNAL: *In all of my life, when have I felt most opposed by Satan? Looking back, can I see possible reasons? What happened?*

He who prays must wage a mighty warfare
against the doubt and murmuring excited by the
faintheartedness and unworthiness we feel within us.

MARTIN LUTHER

The old serpent will tempt you and entice you,
but he will be sent packing by prayer, and if you do some
useful work in the meantime, you will block his chief approach.

THOMAS À KEMPIS

Deliverance

The righteousness of the upright delivers them,
but the unfaithful are trapped by evil desires.

Proverbs 11:6, NIV

Harry Houdini, history's most renowned escape artist and magician, never found a jail cell or bank vault that could hold him. He escaped from a water tank, where he had been suspended upside down, chained and handcuffed, and left for dead. He once escaped from an "escape proof" Washington jail cell that had held a presidential assassin, then let the other prisoners out and locked them up in different cells.

Houdini's feats depended on incredible physical skills and meticulous preparation. But he was caught unprepared once, and it cost him his life. In Montreal for a show in 1926, he was approached backstage by a student who had heard that Houdini could take blows to the stomach without feeling pain. The student, unaware that Houdini always tightened his muscles before doing the trick on stage, landed a couple of hard slugs before Houdini was ready. The resulting internal injury caused an infection. Houdini died a few days later.

We've been talking about Jabez escape strategies all week. I think Jabez would tell Houdini, "Don't even come to the show, Harry, because sooner or later, when you're not quite ready, you'll get caught in your own game."

So, what does it take to catch a Houdini or a Jabez unaware? Not much, really. As our verse today says, the reward of righteous living is that you are delivered from traps. Yet, the record of entrapment in Christian ministry is heartbreaking. A few years ago, Dr. Howard Hendricks of Dallas Seminary set out to study men in full-time ministry who had experienced major moral failures. He found 246 men who had fallen within a two-year period. That's more than ten Jabezes a month going down in flames, some taking a lot of people with them!

My friend, the further you go in your journey, the more protection from temptation matters. Several factors combine to put you at greater risk:

- Your decisions, example, and influence affect more people;
- Your opportunities may leave you spiritually, physically, and emotionally depleted;
- Your successes in significant ministry may convince you that you are less vulnerable instead of more;
- Your accountability to God is greater.

"Beware of no man more than yourself," wrote Charles Spurgeon, "we carry our worst enemies within us." And the more God uses you, the easier it will be for an unspoken lie to slip into your thinking: "God wouldn't let me go down, even if I'm sinning—He needs me and favors me too much." But one day you'll be caught backstage unprepared for a quick jab that could end it all.

I've noticed that when Satan brings a Jabez down, he goes for the most damage possible. The time, the manner, the circumstances—he'll maximize our failures so they cause pain *everywhere.* You know what I'm talking about. You know the untold numbers who won't have anything to do with Christianity because of what their ex-pastor did. That pastor didn't start out to cause pain. He started out to bring blessing. But like Houdini, he fell into a trap of his own making.

The truth is, the farther you go for God, the narrower the road becomes and the harder God will judge you should you fall into serious sin. You've tasted amazing things from His hands, but you can lose it all—for a period of time or for the rest of your life. The grief can be staggering.

I remember trying to minister after I had committed a sin. I felt terrible, but I wanted to press ahead for God. I was sitting on a platform, getting ready to serve an audience as I had always done, when some words dropped into my heart: *You have no idea how worthless you'll be if I take My hand off you.*

I recoiled in shock, and I hope I never recover from that shock.

Join me every day in laying aside entangling sins. Let's walk forward today pursuing God's favor with watchfulness, humility, faithfulness, a clear conscience, and great hope.

MY JABEZ JOURNAL: *In what area of my life am I most likely to make excuses for my sins or routinely presume upon God's grace?*

In a great house there are not only vessels of gold and silver,
but also of wood and clay, some for honor and some for dishonor.
Therefore if anyone cleanses himself from the latter,
he will be a vessel for honor, sanctified and useful for the Master,
prepared for every good work.

2 TIMOTHY 2:20–21

Temptations are tramps; treat them kindly
and they return bringing others with them.

AUTHOR UNKNOWN

Children *of* Light

You were once darkness, but now you are light in the Lord. Walk as children of light (for the fruit of the Spirit is in all goodness, righteousness, and truth), finding out what is acceptable to the Lord.

Ephesians 5:8–10

I work with a young professional (I'll call him Charlie) who once came to a breakthrough moment in his life that looked anything but promising. He described it like this: "In my mind, I'm standing in a dark hallway. Ahead I see light, and that light is my present life. Yet I feel trapped in my past, and I can't walk forward into the light."

I wasn't surprised by Charlie's gloomy picture. Just watching him in recent months, I could tell he was bound up inside over something.

Late one night, we began to talk. Charlie's conversation turned to college and a string of academic failures. Things had turned around dramatically for him when he was diagnosed with Attention Deficit Disorder. After getting on medication, Charlie had left school with straight As. But something was still terribly wrong.

Charlie talked about high school, then junior high. He

chronicled the humiliations and taunting from his peers. He told of all the teachers who wrote him off because they were sure he just wasn't trying. Soon his recollecting had traveled back to third grade. "By third grade, I knew," he said.

"Knew what?" I asked.

"That I would fail. That no matter how hard I try, I *am* a failure."

Charlie's condition had been recognized and treated. But his heart was still in chains. To make his breakthrough, Charlie needed to change his mind about himself. The truth was there, waiting for him to pick it up and own it.

"But I know you," I told him. "The Charlie I know is *not* a failure! You are an achiever. And now I know that you are also a courageous overcomer." Then I asked him to picture himself again in the dark hallway. But this time, I suggested, reach for a switch on the wall, the switch marked "The Truth about Charlie." Flip it on, I said. Tears flowed down Charlie's face.

After a few minutes, I asked, "Are you ready to walk forward now?"

"I'm already starting to walk!" he said.

Do you feel hampered today by sins, failures, or emotional injuries in your past? The truth can set you free. Do you feel burdened by old accusations, like Charlie did? Today's verse tells you that you are a child of the light, and your true freedom is in letting the light of God's truth shine on your life.

As you've been reading through the daily selections this week, you have encountered some huge truths about living free from darkness and defeat. Our discussion has focused specifically on temptation and sin and the pain they cause. But I wonder: Which truths do you still need to pick up?

Here's a recap of what we've learned:

- God wants you to flee temptation, and He wants you to pray daily for protection from it;
- God will provide the way of escape for every temptation that you will ever face;
- You can wisely set about to understand how, why, and when certain recurring sins happen, and you can avoid a lot of temptation by meeting the underlying needs those sins represent in other, God-honoring ways;
- The Holy Spirit is ready to give you the comfort you need so that you will not feel the need to sin at that moment;
- The devil will flee from you if you resist him in God's power;
- The more powerfully God uses you, the more you'll need divine protection from temptation and the enemy's direct attack.

I encourage you to put each of these life-changing truths to work today—deliberately, persistently, and expectantly. You were never meant to spend your days bound up in pain, victimized by temptation, or sabotaged by sin. "Since we have these promises, dear friends," Paul urged, "let us purify ourselves from everything that contaminates body and spirit, perfecting holiness out of reverence for God" (2 Corinthians 7:1, NIV).

I saw Charlie a few days later and asked how he was doing.

"I'm an entirely different person!" he exclaimed. He told me that just that day, God had poured affirmation into his life from dozens of people. "I realize that I'm not that boy trapped in the darkness," he said. "I'm living *now* in the light of the truth!"

That's what God does. When we're ready to pick up the truth and walk forward into the light, He will lead us to a wholeness and personal victory over sin that had seemed impossible only moments before.

My Jabez Journal: *"God, I am a child of light. Show me old parts of my life where I still need to flip on the switch of the truths You're showing me."*

"I am the light of the world. He who follows Me shall not walk in darkness, but have the light of life."

John 8:12

Epilogue

CELEBRATING *the* JABEZ MIRACLE

Without Christ, not one step;
with Him, anywhere.

DAVID LIVINGSTONE

COULD GOD BE THAT GOOD?

And the LORD said, "I will cause all my goodness to pass in front of you, and I will proclaim my name, the LORD, in your presence."

EXODUS 33:19, NIV

How good—I mean, how tender, kind, and giving—do you think God really is? Over the last month, we've spent many days talking about His extraordinary goodness. But I want to help you see today that to continue to reach for the larger life God is bringing you, you must be continually open to being surprised—even shocked—by His lavish generosity. And I don't mean some kind of divine, general goodness toward the world; I mean toward you!

I used to teach at a Christian college. One Monday a very discouraged senior came to my office. She was a straight-A student, a cheerleader, well liked and serious about her walk with the Lord. But she confessed to being lonely and depressed. It took a while for us to get to the sore point: her social life. She hadn't had a date since the previous semester.

"Julie, do you pray?" I asked.

Being a good Bible college student, she was startled. "Of

course, I pray. I'm *required* to pray!"

I pressed further. "What do you pray about?" She started running down her list—missionaries, friends, unsaved in her family, sick people. "But do you ever pray for yourself?" I asked.

"Sure, I pray that I'll be a stronger Christian and be more faithful about—"

I interrupted. "Julie, have you asked God for a date?"

"Oh, Dr. Wilkinson!" she said, rolling her eyes. "God doesn't set up dates!"

"But wait," I said. "You've read the Old Testament. He sent wives, didn't He? He even provided a second husband for Ruth."

Julie sat there stunned. A God who could be that good didn't seem realistic. Still, by the time she had left my office, we had made an agreement. We would both pray every day that God would bring her a date, *and that He would do so by that Friday night.*

I probably looked confident as Julie left that day, but as soon as she was gone, I anxiously phoned home. "Darlene, you'd better start praying!" I said. And I told her about my agreement with Julie.

The next day, a tall senior named Ed walked into my office (you can tell where this story is going!). Ed was very unhappy. He'd asked another girl to marry him, and she'd said no—a definite, please-don't-ask-again no. Ed knew that he'd never be happy again and was thinking of dropping out of school. I thought only briefly about what to say.

"Ed, you need to date other people as soon as possible," I said. "In fact, you need to ask someone out for this Friday night." In one of the more daring acts of faith in my life, I did not mention Julie.

At first the jilted senior balked. But by the time he'd left my office, we also shared an agreement. Ed would try to find a date.

The rest of that week, Darlene and I prayed. Julie prayed. Ed turned his thoughts away from his disappointment and toward Friday night. And God worked.

The next Monday morning on my way across campus, I saw Julie running toward me. Her feet seemed to barely touch the ground. The first thing she wanted to tell me about was her terrific Friday evening date…with a guy named Ed. "You know Ed, don't you?" she asked.

"A little bit," I said, trying not to burst out laughing.

When she was through talking excitedly about her weekend, I asked, "Julie, how do you feel about God?"

She quieted and then began to shake her head in amazement. "You know, I've always believed that God loves me," she said. "But for the first time, I feel that God really *likes* me."

Do you understand that God is *that* good…and He likes you! He wants to answer your big, world-changing prayers, and He longs to meet your most intimate, personal desires too.

A sudden realization of the amazing goodness of God is where the Jabez miracle begins in your life. A daily conviction that *you've tasted only the beginning* is how you keep that miracle growing for the rest of your life.

My Jabez Journal: *Have I experienced God's extravagant goodness recently? Have I been pleading for it?*

For You, Lord, are good, and ready to forgive,
and abundant in mercy to all those who call upon You.

Psalm 86:5

The only limits to prayer are the promises of God
and His ability to fulfill those promises,
"Open thy mouth wide and I will fill it."

E. M. Bounds

WHO, ME?

"Who has made man's mouth? Or who makes the mute, the deaf, the seeing, or the blind? Have not I, the LORD? Now therefore, go, and I will be with your mouth and teach you what you shall say."

EXODUS 4:11–12

Whenever you wonder what God could possibly have been thinking when He called someone like you to such an extraordinary adventure of faith, remember an aging sheepherder with a bad temper and a botched record. His name was Moses. One of the Old Testament's greatest leaders, he was also one of it's most reluctant.

His Jabez story starts in the outback of Midian, a desolate region to the east of the Sinai peninsula. After an earlier, promising start as an adopted son in the courts of Pharoah, things go downhill fast.

One day he happens upon an Egyptian master beating an Israelite. Enraged and thinking no one was looking, Moses kills the Egyptian and buries him in the sand. The next day, when he tries to separate two scuffling Israelites, one of them says, "Who made you ruler and judge over us? Are you thinking of killing me as you killed the Egyptian?" (Exodus 2:14, NIV)

Feeling rejected by his own people and exposed as a murderer, Moses flees. For forty years he hides in the desert herding sheep, a man on the run from failure and shame.

But God still has plans for Moses. One day He speaks to him out of a burning bush, and what He presents is a Jabez-sized proposition: "I will send you to Pharaoh," God says, "that you may bring My people, the children of Israel, out of Egypt" (Exodus 3:10).

In view of his circumstances and his past record, Moses' response is understandable. "Who am I?" he asks. You can almost see his mouth hanging open. God's extraordinary future for him has thrown him into a full-scale identity crisis.

Do you recognize that reflex? God plants a seed in your spirit—an unusual and exciting plan to enlarge your territory for Him. But you see some things that God must have missed. You see, for example, what the "other guys" who succeed seem to have that you don't. You see what it would take in personal sacrifice. You see your own sorry existence, questionable past, difficult personality, and rusty skills....

Why *wouldn't* God's extraordinary plans for you throw you into an identity crisis?

If you look at the account of the conversation between Moses and God (Exodus 3–4), you'll see Moses putting up one objection after another to the destiny God has in mind for him:

- Who am I that I should go?
- Who am I that I should lead?

- Who will I say has sent me?
- What if they don't believe me?

After telling God that his main disqualification is that he's not a good talker, Moses winds up his defense with a desperate plea: "O Lord, please send someone else to do it!"

Still, God persists. And prevails.

I hope you don't dismiss this desert standoff as some kind of Sunday school melodrama complete with plastic sandals, cotton beards, and cardboard cutout sheep. This *is* an identity crisis, and it is the defining moment in Moses' life. You see, all of his questions and concerns are good ones. And all of his feelings of inadequacy are real. Yet after Moses says yes, God uses this shy, reluctant shepherd to accomplish one of the most amazing leadership feats in history.

If you haven't arrived at this kind of turning point yet, you will one day. How do I know? Because to accomplish His miraculous kingdom work through you, God will have to call you past the truth about yourself and show you that what really matters is the truth about Himself. He will tell you, as He did Moses: "I am God." "I am sending you." "My power and presence will go with you." "I will never forsake you."

And that will be the beginning of your new identity—an unlikely hero whose God is strong enough, loving enough, trustworthy enough, and present enough to accomplish anything He calls you to do.

Just in case you ever wonder what God could possibly be thinking when He calls someone like you, read the sheepherder's eloquent farewell speech (the whole book of Deuteronomy). You'll find a man so transformed by a lifetime of seeing what God can do that he doesn't spend a minute bringing up what *he* can or can't do.

MY JABEZ JOURNAL: *What is the biggest endeavor for Him that I could imagine God calling me to? How do I feel about that?*

"And the LORD, He is the One who goes before you.
He will be with you, He will not leave you nor forsake you;
do not fear nor be dismayed."

MOSES TO JOSHUA, HIS SUCCESSOR,
IN DEUTERONOMY 31:8

We do well to remember, before we consign the concept of spiritual leadership to the arena of the superstar, that we serve a God who invaded this planet as a small, fragile baby.

STACY RINEHART

Only he who can see the invisible can do the impossible.

FRANK GAINES

KEEP THIS FOREVER *in* YOUR HEART

"O LORD, God of our fathers Abraham, Isaac and Israel, keep this desire in the hearts of your people forever, and keep their hearts loyal to you."

1 CHRONICLES 29:18, NIV

One night a prince named Solomon reached for the blessed life, and God answered. The prince, as you know from reading your Bible, had everything going for him: a legendary and powerful father, a stable kingdom, and God's favor since his birth.

As a direct result of God's blessings, Solomon became the richest and wisest king in Israel's history. Yet he lived up to only a fraction of his potential. The Bible says that as Solomon aged, "his heart was not fully devoted to the LORD his God" (1 Kings 11:4, NIV). Solomon's reputation even before he died was blighted, and his legacy was marred by material excess, compromise, immorality, and idolatry.

One night, millennia later, a shoe salesman reached for the blessed life, and God answered. His name was Dwight L. Moody.

Sitting in a church service one evening in Chicago, Moody heard a preacher declare that with just one person who was "fully devoted to the Lord," God could shake the world. Dwight Moody decided to be that man.

As a direct result of God's blessings, Moody's preaching led millions to Christ. At the height of Moody's ministry, a journalist sent to interview him came back with a frank report: "I see nothing remarkable in this man." Yet until the day he died, Moody dramatically impacted eternity for Christ. His approach to mass evangelism and personal witnessing affected the course of the church in America and continues to influence evangelists like Billy Graham and Luis Palau.

One day you reached for the blessed life, and God answered. How will your story of miracles and blessings end?

While the blessed life begins with a simple request, it can continue only if our hearts are fully devoted to the Lord. We can start out with the advantages of a prince or the limitations of a shoe salesman—and God will seem to barely notice. What matters is the ongoing, daily sacrifice of our wants and will to Him.

I'm always moved by the example of the apostle Paul. Actually, Paul seems to exemplify both Solomon and Moody in certain ways, being a brilliant and learned Pharisee on the one hand and an ordinary tentmaker by trade on the other. But notice, his legacy for eternity depends on neither!

From the moment Christ called him, Paul never looked back. And the farther on his spiritual journey he traveled, the fewer distractions and compromises he could tolerate. Listen to his testimony near the end of his life:

> *Whatever was to my profit I now consider loss for the sake of Christ.... But one thing I do: Forgetting what is behind and straining toward what is ahead, I press on toward the goal to win the prize for which God has called me heavenward in Christ Jesus. (Philippians 3: 7, 13–14)*

How can you and I keep our hearts devoted and our legacy safe? Learning from Paul's advice, we could summarize a lifelong plan of action into three simple commitments:

- Keep Christ first in our thoughts and actions;
- Press ahead toward God's goal for our lives;
- Let the past go.

When God called you into a larger life for Him and you responded, He had a prize in mind. Go for the prize, my friend, until you draw your last breath! Until the moment you step into eternity, you'll never fully know the dimensions of His generous love and important purpose for you.

Strain toward that day with me—remembering our Lord and our calling in Him and forgetting everything else.

If you and I keep this kind of fierce loyalty to God in our hearts, one day soon we'll be standing before His throne with great anticipation. Next to us will be Jabez and his kin—sheep-herders and shoe salesmen all—eager to welcome us and to hear more amazing stories of the fully devoted life. And together we'll hear God say, "Well done, my good and faithful servants. Enter into the joy of your Lord."

MY JABEZ JOURNAL: *What stories of God's power, protection, and blessing in my life would I most like to celebrate with Jabez throughout eternity?*

The stone the builders rejected has become the capstone;
the LORD has done this, and it is marvelous in our eyes.
This is the day the LORD has made; let us rejoice and be glad in it.

PSALM 118:22–24, NIV

Brothers, think of what you were when you were called. Not many of you were wise by human standards; not many were influential; not many were of noble birth. But God chose the foolish things of the world to shame the wise; God chose the weak things of the world to shame the strong. He chose the lowly things of this world and the despised things—and the things that are not—to nullify the things that are, so that no one may boast before him.

1 CORINTHIANS 1:26–29, NIV

I will go anywhere provided it is forward.

DAVID LIVINGSTONE

Experience the Power of The Prayer That Blessed Jabez

The Prayer of Jabez Bible Study reveals how to make praying the Jabez prayer a lifetime habit. Readers will broaden their understanding of the four components of the Jabez prayer ("bless me, enlarge my borders, keep Your hand upon me, keep me from evil") by investigating key Scripture passages and learning how to apply them to their lives.

ISBN 1-57673-979-1